"When I came on the Department in 1986 everyone soon heard the story
of the Captain at One's. What I like about this book is the reader will see
the personal side of Shakey that made him this legendary firefighter.
It's good stuff."

— Chief Victor Conley, Chief of Irving, Texas; Fire Chief of the Year 2013 by
TFCA; Safety Award 2018 by TFCA for Blocker Program

"Captain Shakey Holder, as one who worked with him,
he is the real thing. This book captures the personal side of Shakey,
of all his amazing life experiences that formed him into the father, friend
and firefighter he came to be. I'm glad I got to work with him
and thoroughly enjoyed reading his story."

— Chief "Rusty" Wilson, Fire Chief of Mesquite, Texas;
Texas Fire Chief of the year 2017

"Billy Gene Holder, better know as Shakey is my best friend
and greatest firefighter to ever put on a set of bunker pants.
I'm glad he has his own book about his life.
It would do well for everyone to know about this great man."

— Retired Irving Firefighter Travis Eden
and author of *Firefighter ll In Angels Hands*

THE LEGENDARY STORY OF

SHAKEY

The Oldest Known Firefighter to Work on a Front-Line Engine Company on a Paid Department in the United States

clif clifton

ISBN: 978-1-962402-80-4 (hardcover)
978-1-962402-81-1 (paperback)

Cover photo credit: Tom Pennington,
Getty Images Staff Photographer, *Ft Worth Star Telegram* photographer

Published by

Fideli Publishing, Inc.
119 W. Morgan St.
Martinsville, IN 46151
www.FideliPublishing.com

DEDICATED TO

Jim Presnall, who died in the line of duty on February 28, 1984, in an apartment fire truss roof collapse. Jim was in my rookie class in 1981.

Wendal "Pooh" McCluer, who died in the line of duty on January 25, 1988, working on the highway. I relieved Pogh each morning on Truck 7.

Steve "Stevie" Grothe, who passed away from cancer after retirement. Stevie and I began our career the same day, June 25, 1981, C-Shift.

All my other brother firefighters who are battling cancer now or have lost their battle with cancer.

TABLE OF CONTENTS

Acknowledgements vii

Author's Note ix

Introduction xi

The Early Years 1

Time to Get the Heck Out of Cartwright 11

Moving to Irving 18

The Fire Department Interview 23

Waiting for the Call 26

What's In a Name? 32

Success in Everything but One Thing 37

Herding the Chickens 43

Larry Holder 47

Rick Holder 56

Cindy Holder Jeffery 62

What You See Is What You Get 69

I'm Going to Change Your Life 74

The Truck 83

Running with the Bulls 87

Millionaire Twice Over and Over and Over 94

The "C" Word 97

Lee Pollei 108

Don Burrows 114

Mike "Stick" Worthington 120

Jin Lee 127

Matt Smith 134

Ronnie Mayo 139

Calvin Morris 147

Thoughts from the Heart 151

    Josh Holder, Shakey's Oldest Grandson 153

    Austin Jeffery, Shakey's Grandson 156

    Julie Gauthier Marquett, Ginger's Daughter 159

    Robby Gauthier, Ginger's Son 160

    Nick Holder, SHAKEY's Grandson 162

    Kagan Duffy, Shakey's Grandson 164

    Kelly Markham, Family Friend 165

    Garret Jeffery, Shakey's Grandson 167

    Jim Caudle, Irving Firefighter 169

    Ronnie Yankey, Retired Captain, Irving Fire Dept. 170

    Amanda, Shakey's Granddaughter 172

    Earl Yarbrough, Friend 173

    Dr. Perkins, Shakey's Oncologist 175

    Jean Hicks, Ginger's Best Friend 176

    Endnotes 180

About the Author 181

ACKNOWLEDGEMENTS

To Shakey's family, I want to thank you for your dad and Ginger giving me this opportunity to see my dream of writing a book come to fruition. Your patience with me, as I learned how to compose yours and Shakey's words into a book is greatly appreciated. The bond of friendship that was built between us is the most rewarding thing, I think happened and what I cherish the most. Thank you again.

To my wife, you are the best. You have been my soulmate for 52 years and I pray for many more. Thank you for your patience this past year, your help with frustrating computer problems and for allowing me to go write many evenings at the coffee shop. I love you. hi.

To Lynda McCallum, I know you want no recognition, but your friendship and servant's heart to help me through the good times and bad times is a gift to me from our God. Thank you for all the encouragement over the years and typing, not only, this book, but all my poems and my other books. I could not have done it without your help. I love you.

To my sister, Donna, and friend, Dave Holland, for all the encouragement and thoughts on the book. I greatly appreciate it and love you. Dave, I hope to see you at Aw Shucks, Tuesday. It's my time to buy a bowl of shrimp cocktail.

AUTHOR'S NOTE

Gene "Shakey" Holder's wife, Ginger, had a dream of honoring her husband by having a book written about his life. They didn't want a biography, but a story of his life and the stories that he loves to tell. At the age of 89, Shakey's mind is sharp as a tack, and he is on the go all the time as you will see when you read the book.

Shakey and I worked for the Irving Fire Department and there is an annual fish fry every September that we both attend. For several years at the fish fry, Ginger would ask me who could write their book. Long story short, finally I agreed to take on the (ad)venture. Our agreement was I would write their book and learn how to publish and in return they would pay for the publishing of my book, *Real Stories of Real Heroes of the IFD,* that I began after I retired. This allowed me to begin this incredible journey, interviewing Shakey, his amazing family and our dedicated fellow fire fighters over this past year for this memorable book, *Shakey.*

Note: I use Gene's given name until the point in his story where he earned the nickname "Shakey."

INTRODUCTION

Urban legend (sometimes contemporary legend, modern legend, urban myth, or urban tale): a genre of folklore comprising stories or fallacious claims circulated as true, especially as having happened to a "friend of a friend" or a family member, often with horrifying, humorous, or cautionary elements. These legends can be entertaining but often concern mysterious peril or troubling events, such as disappearances and strange objects or entities.[1]

Captain Gene "Shakey" Holder of the Irving Fire Department in Texas, who is not an urban legend but a real legend, began his career with the Irving Fire Department in December 1955 at the age of 21. He worked for 56 years, retiring at the age of 77—NOT at a desk job, but on an engine company in South Irving. For most of those years, he served at Station 1, the only single company house in Irving (meaning a single apparatus at the station), and with a three-person crew for a good deal of his time there. The engine company also had to make all ambulance calls in their District, adding to their workload, until the department finally added an ambulance in 2016.

Though small in stature, Gene Holder was a fighter his entire life. It began with a fight when he was six years old. Fighting all through his high school years. Fighting to get out of Cartwright to find a good paying job. Fighting to provide for his family with three small children on a meager firefighter's salary, working a 24-hours-on and 24-hours-off schedule. Fighting fires with a fire hose and tank water and not much else in the early years of his career. Fighting the struggles of undiagnosed dyslexia late into his fire career. Fighting his superiors for his rights and the rights of the men who worked with him. Fighting stage four cancer at the age of 70. Fighting the aftereffects of this cancer for the past 19 years. Fighting COVID-19 for a month in the hospital while I was writing this story.

Gene is a fighter and a whole lot more as you will see as you read the story of Shakey, the oldest known firefighter to work on a front-line engine company on a paid department in the United States.

THE EARLY YEARS

Zoro (Corky) Holder in front of rough cut lumber house.

The year was 1934, and a baby boy came into the world kicking and fighting. His parents were Clinton Lafayette and Gracie Mae Holder, and they lived in a rural area in Grayson County, Texas, on the Texas/Oklahoma border. Clinton held his newborn son in his arms, wondering what kind of man he would become. The baby's mother, still lying in bed, asked to have her son back in her arms. Clinton sat down beside her, and as they stared at their baby boy, they hoped for a better life someday with him.

Both were worried about how they would be able to feed another mouth in the family. This was because the world was in the economic disaster called the Great Depression that began with the stock market crash in 1929. Two years earlier, boll weevils destroyed most of the cotton crop and the farmers began to grow other crops to prevent another economic disaster. Peanuts became a leading crop for the area, but hard times continued.

All these efforts to survive were wiped out by the Dust Bowl that came to the Central Plains of the United States, including Oklahoma and Texas. It was caused by an excessive heat wave, severe drought conditions and the poor farming methods used at this time. Major dust storms had blown away the topsoil, causing many families to suffer through hard times.

The federal government was implementing new programs to help ease the suffering of its citizens all over the country. Thankfully, there were a lot of new work opportunities in Grayson County, Texas, and Bryan County, Oklahoma, because the WPA (Works Progress Administration) was building the new Denison Dam for Lake Texoma.

Controversy

Two major controversies occurred for Oklahomans and Texans during these years. The first controversy was the German prisoners of war from World War II, who were used to help build the dam, apparently taking jobs from Americans.

The second controversy almost led into a Civil War between Oklahoma and Texas. In July 1931 a new free bridge was opened over the Red River. A toll bridge operating nearby filed a lawsuit for not being compensated for the lost revenue they were promised. Texas Governor Ross Sterling ordered the new bridge to be barricaded while they settled the dispute. Oklahoma Governor William Murray claimed the bridge both began and ended in Oklahoma and that the Texas governor needed to take down the barricades. Texas Rangers were sent to the conflict and

Governor Murray, with a pistol in his hand, led the Oklahoma soldiers who were sent to the conflict.

The press descended upon the area and described the conflict as the Red River Bridge War. It lasted for several weeks. People suffering because of the Depression thought it was a farce, but the new bridge did bring some new economic growth for Cartwright businesses and bars. (Wikipedia, https://en.wikipedia.org/wiki/Red_River_Bridge_War)

Texans began coming to Cartwright because the counties where they lived prohibited the sale of alcohol, and lots of beer joints were opening in the unincorporated community of Cartwright. The city was named after Congressman Wilburn Cartwright. Texas cowboys and personnel from Perrin Air Force Base came by the droves to buy and drink beer in the local beer joints popping up along Main St.

Another interesting fact about this area was that Oklahoma had a no-wait period for marriage licenses. Texans wanting to get married quickly, would drive up U.S. Hwy. 69/75 through Cartwright to obtain a marriage license certificate in Durant, Oklahoma. New businesses continued popping up along the dirt roads to take care of the growing community, but all Clinton and Gracie's thoughts were on how to provide for their three young children.

Our Family Did All Right

The baby was the third of seven children. The first child's name was Zoro. Clinton wanted to name the new baby, Lastro, but after a bit of persistence by Gracie, they named him Billy Gene Holder, after her favorite actor and war hero, Gene Autry. As Gene got older, friends of his mother would say he even looked like Gene Autry.

In my interview with Gene, he quipped, "We all looked like Indians; we have Chickasaw blood and Gene Autry's mother was Mississippi Choctaw." In 1831-32 the U.S. government began relocating both the Choctaw and Chickasaw nations from the American south into Bryan

County. Southern aristocrat and mixed-blood entrepreneur Robert M. Jones, one of the wealthiest men in the Choctaw Nation, owned cotton plantations in the rich bottomland in this area. During the Civil War, Confederate General Albert B. Pike established Fort McCulloch in Bryan County and occupied it with more than 1,000 American Indian troops. No Civil War engagements occurred in Bryan County. (https.//www.okhistory.org>entry)

Gene continued, "My great-great-grandma was Chickasaw, and her name was Comanche Straight. When the government began paying the Indians money, she tried to get on the rolls to acquire her benefits. The government shipped her to Oklahoma before she got her registration number, and she died on the way to Oklahoma. We didn't get any of the government benefits because she never got her roll number. My family did alright, though. They built the first schoolhouse in Grayson County. The Holder schoolhouse is still out there, at Lloyd Lake on Highway 75."

Learned to Work

Gene continued, "My grandfather Hudgins was a drop-off baby from a town in Kentucky, where someone left him in a basket on a doorstep. I always asked my mother how they knew his name was Hudgins. She would always say, 'I guess they wrote the name Hudgins on a piece of paper and left it in the basket.'

"The family that took him in didn't treat him as their own child. They worked him, and were always mean to him, so at the age of 12, he ran off and came to Texas. There he met his first wife, my grandmother, who was not a saint! She was also mean to him and to their kids—she wouldn't give her kids any money. They all had to work from a young age if they wanted anything, and it made my granddad the way he was. He knew he had to work for what he wanted, and he taught my dad the same work ethic. Grandpa was able to have a nice farm and he was a hard worker all his life. At the age of 80, I saw him jump up and touch his toes."

Gene inherited his grandfather's traits. He knew how to work hard and did some extraordinary things. Gene often said, "I was successful in everything I did, in my entire life, except for one thing."

Granddad Found a Good Wife

Gene told me this story about his granddad. "When his first wife died, he remembered the girl that he liked when he lived with her parents in Kentucky. She was always there to talk to when her parents mistreated him. She was his only friend growing up, and he decided to go back to Kentucky and try to find her. He was determined. Think about it. This was in the days before the internet; you could not look up people online. He went around town, asking about her and after a long search, he finally found her. Her husband had also died, so he proposed to her and brought her back to Texas. They married and my granddad had a good life with her, and all the family really liked her."

Don't Give Up!

Gene was small in stature, but his father instilled a strong work ethic in him. Growing up poor, he and his brothers and sisters had to help in any way they could to survive. There were times they didn't own a car and had to go to town in a wagon pulled by their horse.

When Gene was six years old, he and his siblings would pick cotton for 25 cents a day in those hot Oklahoma summers. "We were always moving. When Dad would hear about work, he would pack everything we owned in the truck and go find another place to live. Once we lived in an empty grocery store. It was open-concept living, no-walls and all nine of us living together in that store.

"Before I was twelve, we lived in a tent along the river. We also lived in Granddad's barn with dirt floors. My father told me once, 'When you leave home, the world will be easy for you.'"

What his dad meant was all the hard work Gene had to do as a child and young adult prepared him to persevere when times were tough. And there were tough times in his life. His parents had prepared him not just to survive but to be successful in life. Gene said, "My dad would always say, 'Don't give up; keep working hard.'"

Gene did and he saw the fruits of his upbringing and labor. These qualities allowed him to have an incredibly good life, provide for his family and have a tremendous impact on many, many people's lives.

Be Smarter Than the Cows

Gene reminisced about when he was a little kid, he had to go to the field and lead their one cow back to the house to be milked. On the way to the house, he had to pass a general store that also sold minnows to fishermen.

"I was only in the sixth grade, and the cow was thirsty. I couldn't keep that cow from drinking from that minnow tank. The owner of the store would get mad, yelling at me, 'Your cow is eating my minnows.' Gene said, "There's no way that my cow was eating those minnows."

Gene knew he had to do something to keep that cow out of the minnow tank, so he went home and told his dad what was happening. His dad told him, "Son, you got to be smarter than the cow."

Gene knew the cow was stronger than him, and he couldn't keep him out of the minnow tank, so he found some strands of barbed wire and nailed it across the opening leading up to the store. Gene said, "It kept that cow from drinking from that tank." He remembered that lesson throughout his life—that he had to be smarter than the cows he was leading.

Struggles

"When we moved around like we did, it was hard. Each time we moved, I had to go to a new school, where I got picked on. The school bully would come and pick on me as the new kid, and the other kids would egg him on, and he would punch me. I learned how to defend myself. That's how those days were...kids picking on each other. I had to start fighting early in life. As I got older, I struggled in school, flunked the fifth grade three times. I self-promoted myself to the sixth grade," recalled Gene.

He had dyslexia, which made reading very difficult for him. He didn't like to read, even to this day. Test taking was also hard for him because he read so slowly. It was frustrating, but Gene learned he just had to try harder than everyone else and that's what he did.

At the age of 12 he began working in one of the bars in Cartwright, carrying cases of beer to customers' trucks and cleaning up their messes inside the bar. "Those cowboys would come to Cartwright and get drunk and spend all their money on beer and not on their family," said Gene. "From a young age I saw how drinking ruins people's lives."

He paused and remarked, "Geez, I saw a bunch of drunk cowboy fights while working there. I also knew the grocery store owner, Betty. Her store was just down the street from where I worked, she always liked me and saw how hard I worked. Her son, Johnny, was my best friend and we got in a lot of fights." (Betty would have a huge impact later in Gene's adult life.)

These struggles—being picked on and struggling in school—gave Gene a heart for the underdog. His whole life, he would fight for them, helping them financially when they needed a helping hand, teaching what his dad taught him—how to be successful, by hard work, but not by being coddled. It gave Gene great satisfaction to see the many he helped overcome their struggles financially and become successful in life.

First House

Gene continued his story. "Mom inherited $25 when her mother died. She took the money and bought a lot in Cartwright, and Dad built us a house with rough-cut lumber.

"The lumber mill would saw these trees for lumber. They would pile up the edges of the trees with the bark still on them and give them away for free. Dad took the truck, and all us kids loaded all it could carry and hauled it back to the house. They were all different sizes, the bark still on them. Dad stood them up and built us a house with a roof, without any 2x4s. Then he wrapped it with tar paper to keep the air from blowing through it. One time a big windstorm came and blew most of the house down. Margie [Gene's younger sister] went over to the front door and closed it. That's about all that was left of the house was the wall with the door on it."

First Love

The Holder family could now settle down in Cartwright and their kids could have a permanent school to attend. Gene was popular in school, but a particular freshman caught his eye. Her name was Ruby. She was three years younger than him, and one day he went up to her in school, wanting to ask her for a date.

Gene recalled, "I asked her if she would go out with me, and she said she would. Later someone told me the only reason she went out with me was because I had a nice car. But we dated all through high school."

Gene was working all the time at various jobs, but whenever he got off from work, he would drive over to Ruby's house and pick her up. He said, "We would drive somewhere, and I would buy her something nice, or go to a movie. We were just kids having fun while in high school."

Break Up

"I graduated and started working in Denison. And Ruby was having her 16th birthday party at her house down outside of town in the Red River bottoms. So, I had gone and bought her a dress to give to her. I went and picked up Charles Taylor, my buddy I worked with in Denison, and he went with me out to the party. When we got there,

Ruby was hanging out with about four boys that lived out there close to her. "Charles said, 'Ruby is acting like she doesn't even like you.' I said, 'Shoot, she don't like me. Let's get out of here.' So, we left, and Ruby and I broke up for about two years after that."

Harry Hines Blvd.

Cindy, who was listening to her dad talk about her mother said, "Dad, the reason Ruby didn't have any boyfriends, you beat them all up."

"Maybe I did, I don't remember," Gene replied. "I do remember a boyfriend we called Harry Hines. We called him that because we had been down on Harry Hines in Dallas and saw how all the boys down there would holler from their cars at the girls 'walking' the streets. He and his friends would drive around Denison hollering at people.

"Four of us got off work at ten o'clock from the 7-Up plant. We jumped in my car, and we went and got us a hot dog and a root beer. These guys drove by where we were parked and hollered, 'You bunch of hillbillies; you need to get back to Cartwright.'

"I turned to Charles and asked, 'Who is that hollering?'

"'That's Harry Hines, who's been dating Ruby.'

"'No kidding.'

"'Gene, they are trying to run you out of town.'

"I stopped my car and got out, and Harry Hines yelled at me, 'I hear you think you are pretty tough.'

"I yelled back, 'I hear you think you are Ruby's boyfriend.'

"The guy got in my face with one of those stare downs, but I reared back and hit him hard in the face. He fell backward, and I hit him a couple more times. You could tell he didn't know how to fight, so I punched him hard again and he took off running across a field. I never was that fast a runner, so I yelled, 'I'll be looking for you.'

I wasn't trying to get Ruby back; I was just defending my honor … not running me out of town!"

Back Together

"I was making good money at the 7 Up company, so I sold the '41 Chevy and got a newer car. Ruby had two cousins who were good looking and lived in Denison, and I would let them borrow my new car while I was at work. At 10 o'clock they would come pick me up, and I would take them home. When Ruby found out I had a new car, her cousins let her come in my car and pick me up. I knew then she wanted to get back together."

The romance was back on, and Gene was happy.

TIME TO GET THE HECK OUT OF CARTWRIGHT

Gene in front of 7UP bottling plant

The phrase "get out of Dodge" came from the "wicked little town" of Dodge City, Kansas. There were a lot of gunfights between the buffalo hunters and cowboys who came into town to enjoy the saloons and brothels. The town hired lawmen like Wyatt Earp and Bat Masterson to keep the peace. The setting for the 1950s TV show, "Gunsmoke," was Dodge City. Marshall Matt Dillon and Kitty would keep the peace with their words—most of the time. Kitty also had her "way" of smoothing things over. They had Deputy Festus' eye on all the trouble in town. I can hear Marshall Dillon saying, "Move on and get out of Dodge."[2]

Drunken Cowboys

Gene was a man who, like Wyatt Earp and Marshall Dillon, never backed down from a fight. Cartwright, Oklahoma, was a lot like Dodge City. Gene told us, "When I was a kid growing up, there were 23 beer joints in a half-mile stretch on Main Street and a grocery store. My brother owns a beer joint there now. He opens it only when he wants to drink. "

Gene continued, "If you wanted to drink, you either had to go to Dallas or Oklahoma City. (Grayson County and Smith County were dry back then—no beer sales allowed.) Cartwright was the closest place for those Texans to buy beer. Those drunk cowboys would flood in there and fill those bars up. I started working there when I was 12 years old. They paid me 25 cents an hour, and I saw a bunch of fights between drunk cowboys."

The Legend Takes Root

Gene's first fight was at the age of six. A boy who was older than Gene was always picking on him. One day, Gene finally had enough and pushed the kid back and falling to the ground, they started wrestling.

"My oldest brother, Corky, came over, and I told him, 'Hold the kid down for me.' When he did, I grabbed a handful of sand and poured it in his eyes. I let him up, and the boy ran off. That boy never picked on me again. Corky went home and told our dad that I didn't know who to fight. He told him, 'He fights boys even I can't beat up.'"

Gene had fights all through his years in school, no matter the size of the kid. "For the most part, my fights were because kids were being picked on, and I didn't like it, so I took up for the kid," Gene said.

Even after high school, Gene had lots of fights. "I remember I had a fight with a guy they said was the toughest man in Denison. I was working at the Beach Stand. It was a bar at Burns Run on Lake Texoma. This guy was drunk and started mouthing me, so I went out there to fight him.

"My buddy, Johnny, had some brass knucks, and he said, 'If the guy starts getting the better of you, I'll hit him with these knucks.' As we went out from behind the bar, a guy sucker punched him and knocked him out without him throwing a punch.

"So, I'm by myself and I go face the guy and punch the guy real hard on the jaw. He fell between the parked cars, and I jumped on him and began punching him. He couldn't get up because the cars were too close together. I knocked the guy out and getting up, yelled, 'You better get out of town and go back to Denison.' The crowd started yelling, 'Gene knocked out the toughest fighter in Denison.' I got a big name for myself for it, by knocking out the toughest fighter in Denison."

Ginger added, "When I was teaching school, a teacher found out I was dating Gene. She said, 'I know him. He's a fighter; he knocked out the toughest guy in Denison.'"

The legend began to grow.

Bold Move

Gene knew for him to succeed he would have to leave Cartwright to find stable work that paid better. His dad had prepared him to do whatever it took to succeed, so he made the bold move to leave. At the age of 19, he went to Denison, Texas, an eight-mile drive across the Red River, which separated the two states, to look for a job. He applied for a job at the 7 Up bottling plant and after they looked at his resume and references, they hired him. He was finally making good money, $1 an hour, which allowed him to pay for the '41 Chevrolet he had bought.

The car had cost $635, and the bank gave him a loan without his dad co-signing the note. He had earned a good reputation around town for his strong work ethic, a reputation that would pay big dividends throughout his life. He paid the down payment on his new car with money he earned working all through high school.

Gene's friend, Charles, also got a job at the plant, and they began commuting back and forth each day, with Charles paying him 25 cents a week for gas money. The bold move to find work in Texas was paying off for Gene.

Standoff at the OK Corral

Things were good until another man, the town bully (TB), who lived outside Cartwright, had lost his ride to work. He worked at the Dr Pepper plant that was close to the 7 Up plant. TB was desperate to find a ride, and someone told him that a guy from Cartwright who drove that '41 Chevy' was working at the 7 Up plant. After work, TB walked over to the parking lot, finding Gene about to get in his car. He walked up to Gene and said, "I lost my ride, and you are going to take me back and forth to work."

Gene looked at TB and demanded, "I will, if you pay me." TB, who was older and much bigger than Gene, puffed up his chest and said, "I'm not paying you no money; I'm riding for free."

Gene stood his ground, fist clenched. "You're not riding with me."

"I am too, and I'm not paying."

"Buddy, you're going to have to walk back home," yelled Gene.

"I've not walked on this ground for three years."

As a small crowd gathered, Gene asked, "How have you done that?"

"By walking on SOBs like you!"

Gene threw the first punch and clocked TB in the jaw. The crowd gathered around them with shouts of approval as the two combatants beat each other up. Gene, now on his knees coughing up blood, saw TB climb in the back seat of his car.

Charles tried to help Gene up, but Gene pushed him away. He told Charles, "Get in. I'm taking this SOB to his house." Gene backed out, spun his tires, and hauled TB home.

As he crossed the Red River, Gene began to think about what his dad had taught him. He remembered his dad saying, "Son, you have to stand up for what you believe in." He had but lost the fight. They got to the railroad tracks, and Gene pulled over to let TB out of his car as he yelled, "If you ride with me, you are going to pay me."

Slamming the car door, TB yelled, "I ain't paying no one to ride." When he got home, Gene took a long hot bath and went to bed. He hurt all over. As he tossed and turned in bed, he thought, *what can I do not to get whooped again?* Finally, he drifted off to sleep.

Round Two

The next day it was raining, and Gene picked up Charles and headed to work. As they left out of town, they saw TB standing on the side of the road waving his hands back and forth for Gene to pick him up.

Charles asked Gene, "Are you stopping?"

"Nope," said Gene, as he drove right by TB with a wry smile on his face and drove to Denison. Gene pulled into the parking lot, parked his car, and walked in to work. All the guys who had witnessed the beating the day before were all staring at him, marveling that he could show up for work. Both plants were yakking about the fight and wondering if there would be round two.

The workday ended and everyone was clocking out, heading to the parking lot and hoping to see another fight. Gene clocked out, walked up to TB, looked up to him, and said, "I told you if you ride, you are going to pay."

TB growled, "You want your ass kicked again? You better give me a ride."

The larger crowd from the day before had gathered and chose up sides for the fight. Gene stood his ground, fists clenched, and declared, "If you kick my ass, then I will give you a ride." Gene ducked the first punch, but with each punch and shout from the crowd, TB kicked Gene's ass, again.

Gene was so tired from the drumming; he could hardly get off the ground. TB, tired and bleeding from his mouth crawled into the back seat. Charles and a couple of his friends from the plant helped Gene up, brushed him off, and said, "You're one tough SOB." They helped Gene into the car, and he drove TB and Charles home without a word said.

The next morning TB was standing on the side of the road, and Gene didn't stop, leaving him there with his arms waving and shouting, "You SOB!" Gene, with another wry smile on his face, drove down to Denison and went to work. After work he saw TB was waiting at his car. A larger crowd from the day before began to gather for round three. It was like an old Gene Autry Western with more than 40 cowboys waiting for the showdown. There were even route drivers from both plants who had heard about the fights and finished their routes early to see the "sheriff and the outlaw" square off.

Gene was looking out the bay door of the plant as his supervisor walked over to him. He put his arm around Gene and said, "He's out there again. You are going to give him a ride out of town?" Gene could only say, "I'm getting tired, tired of getting my ass kicked." Gene slowly walked across the street to the parking lot a whole lot sore from the previous fights, but ready to stand his ground.

TB had climbed into the back seat of Gene's '41 Chevrolet. Gene snarled, "Get out of my damn car!"

"Are we going to do this again?" asked TB, reluctantly opening the door.

"EVERY DAY."

TB grudgingly got out of the car and slammed the car door shut. Gene put his fists up, rocking back and forth, and ready to fight. There's a short stare down with Gene looking TB right in his eyes. TB dropped his arms to his side, turned and started walking toward the schoolyard, mumbling, "This just ain't worth it."

The crowd was disappointed, but Gene sure wasn't. He was just glad he didn't get his ass kicked, and Gene's legend continued to grow.

All Amazed

We were all in Gene's living room—his son, Rick, Ginger, and me, listening to Gene tell his stories like it was yesterday. We were all laughing and marveling how tough Gene was against a bigger man.

Gene said, "He was tough, and I thought I was tough. The dumb thing is he only had to pay me 25 cents a week. I had all those men out there looking at us … at me … to see what I was going to do. Was I going to be a man and stand up for what I believed in?"

"You have to stand up for what you believe in; this is what my dad taught me. I taught that to my kids and all the men who worked for me at the fire department. If one of my firefighters thought he was right, then stand up and change what I told you to do, but you better be right. Better be right," Gene said a second time with emphasis.

"I did that all my life, especially at the fire department. I stood up for what I thought was right, stood up for my firefighters. I had to write a bunch of memos to the Chief because I stood up for what I thought was right. That's how I lived."

"That wasn't much of a life when that guy beat you up every day," Ginger said.

"Now, that's a whole different story," replied Gene.

Soon after this it was time for Gene to move to Texas and go see Ruby, who was living in Dallas—and to get the heck out of Cartwright, Oklahoma.

MOVING TO IRVING

Gene bought a ring and proposed to Ruby after she had graduated from high school. Ruby wanted a better life than Cartwright could offer her and decided she needed to go to Dallas and find a good paying job. Her sister, Caroline, who was living in Pleasant Grove, a suburb of Dallas, said Ruby could live with her until she got back on her feet and Gene and her could be married.

Gene, now 21, decided it was time for him to "fly the chicken coop" and move to Texas to find work and be close to Ruby. He gave his two weeks' notice at the 7 Up plant and at the end of the two weeks he went to his boss's office and thanked him for giving him a job and for all he did for him. He then drove to his parents' house and told them and his two younger brothers, it was time for him to head to Dallas to find work and to be closer to Ruby. He cleaned out his few belongings from his room and pitched them in the back seat of his car. He said his goodbyes and "flew the coop."

Driving Memory Lane

One day after one of our interviews ended, Gene said, "Clif, I want you and your wife to go with me and Ginger to Cartwright. You need to see all these places I'm talking about." So, we set a day to go, and Patti and I drove to McKinney to their home. Patti and Ginger got in the back seat, and I climbed in the front seat with Gene. Gene started the car and headed to Hwy. 75. As he drove (over the speed limit most of the time) to Cartwright, he told me more of his stories. Our first stop was at Grayson County Frontier Village, where the historical society relocated the Holder School House, then to all the other places Gene thought of as he left for Dallas. It was a great day and it helped me write **Driving Memory Lane**.

Gene and Clif.

As Gene drove down Main Street, he thought of all the escapades and fights he had had and the people he had grown up with and ran around with. As he drove by the grocery store, he thought of Bonnie and her son Johnny, who got him into a lot of fights. He recalled what a nice person Bonnie was to him and his family.

As he turned south on Hwy 91 and crossed the railroad tracks, he thought of that tough son of gun TB and hoped he had grown up. Driving through Denison, he circled past the 7 Up plant and saw that old pecan tree by the parking lot where he gave those boys a show, fighting a much bigger opponent. Then he drove past the railroad depot, wishing he had ridden on a train somewhere exciting and thinking maybe someday he could travel the world. Then past all the hangouts he used to cruise with friends. The memories flooded his mind, but now he had to focus on new plans. Through each small town on the 87-mile drive to Dallas he was dreaming of a better life for him and Ruby.

Fresh Start

Gene's sister Betty and her husband, Homer, had moved to Irving and bought a home on Wanda Street for them and their three children. Gene had asked her if he could live with them until he could afford a house. Gene had helped them several times when they were in a difficult spot financially. Betty and Homer knew it would be tight for them, but they agreed to let Gene move in and help him get a fresh start in Texas.

In 1955 there were a lot of opportunities for work in the Dallas/Ft. Worth metroplex, and Irving was in the center of the explosive growth. It was rapidly becoming a distribution center for goods, with the railroad running between Dallas and Ft. Worth. And it didn't take long for Gene to find work.

First Job in Texas

That first night, Betty told Gene where the unemployment agency was, and he should start there looking for work. He got ready for bed, exhausted and fell asleep. The next morning, after a cup of coffee and some Cream of Wheat, Gene drove over to the agency. They told him to apply at O'Keith and Meredith, that they were hiring.

Gene drove over to their offices and after hearing all his work experience, they hired him on the spot. They gave him directions to the warehouse, off Main St. and Irving Boulevard. Gene found his way to the warehouse and met the foreman. He explained to Gene how he wanted the stoves unloaded and stacked, gave him a handcart and put him to work.

Unloading stoves from rail boxcars and stacking them in the ware-house was difficult for Gene. He weighed only 136 pounds, almost the same weight as a crated stove. The foreman admired how hard Gene worked, but finally after a few days working, said he was going to have to let him go before he got hurt. Gene finished the day and went home to tell Ruby and Betty the bad news.

Want You to Stay

This didn't stop Gene. He went back the next day to the unemploy-ment agency and found a job in Dallas working on a golf course. It was Brookhaven Golf Course, off Harry Hines, an A. W. Tillinghast design and one of the most historic golf courses in Texas. Gene found himself shoveling sand all day into a screen and sifting rocks from the sand for the bunkers located on the course. He worked there for a while shoveling sand all day, every day, until he heard of a better job in White Settlement in Tarrant County. He told his employer he was quitting.

They responded, "We want you to stay."

Gene said, "I thought this was a temporary job."

To which they replied, "It is for most people, but not for you."

Gene laughed and thanked them for hiring him, but he had a bet-ter job waiting for him in White Settlement. His parents' upbringing of always working hard continued to serve him well in Texas.

Driving to White Settlement

Gene took the job in White Settlement at Convar Air, a 35-mile drive one way. His sister was helping Gene occasionally with some gas money, and Gene hated it. The two of them were talking one night, and Gene said, "I need to find a job in Irving and stop that driving to Ft. Worth."

"I saw in the newspaper today that Irving was hiring firefighters," said Betty.

"No kidding. I'm going downtown, *today,* and get me an application."

"I went today and got one for you,"

Gene thanked her, and later that night he sat down and filled out the application in his bedroom.

100 Applications

The next day the drive to White Settlement didn't seem that bad. He had the fire department application sitting right there beside him on the car seat, and he planned to take it to the fire station after work.

He clocked out, took a deep breath, walked to his car, and drove back to Irving. Gene parked his car in the parking lot of Central Fire Station and walked into the Station. Gene was met by Lee King, a firefighter who was working that day. They shook hands and Gene said, "I've got my application for a job as a firefighter with me.

Lee reached out his hand to grab the application, and Gene handed it to him. Lee, looking over the application, said, "I'll go put this with the other 100 applications we've gotten."

They talked a bit more, and, as he reached out his hand to shake Lee's hand goodbye, Gene said, "Well, I'll just have to wait for the call from the chief for my interview."

Driving home he began to dream what it would be like to be an Irving firefighter.

THE FIRE DEPARTMENT INTERVIEW

The day came for Gene's interview. Ruby and his sister wished him luck. "We know you can do this, Gene. Just be yourself, and we will see you when you get home," Betty said.

Walking to his car, Gene knew his life could change, if he got this job. He drove over to City Hall and parked his car, and after getting out of his car, he crossed Second Street. Walking up to the glass door, he grabbed the handle and opened it. Stepping in, he stared up the stairway for a moment, hoping the chief would give him a chance at a new life. As he climbed the stairs to the chief's office, a secretary came out of the city manager's office and asked Gene if she could help him.

"I'm here for my interview to become a firefighter," replied Gene.

"You must be Gene Holder."

"Yes, I'm Gene Holder."

She had him take a seat, and Gene nervously watched her walk down the hall and knock on the open door. She stuck her head in and said, "Gene Holder is here for his interview." She then turned and waved for Gene to come, and with a smile, she let him in and closed the door.

The city manager stood and greeted Gene with a handshake, and said, "Gene, I'm John Stiff. Have a seat."

Where Is the Chief?

After some small talk, the city manager said, "Looking at your application, I see you have an Oklahoma driver's license. How long have you been in Texas?"

"About three months."

"Why haven't you gotten your Texas license and plates?"

"Well, I just been waiting, but I'll get them."

"You know you are supposed to get them within 10 days of moving here."

"Yeah, I know; I'm going to do it. I just don't have the money to get them. I came down here to get married to a girl from back home."

"When did you get married?"

"We haven't married, yet. Waiting, maybe to get this job before we do."

"What were you doing back in Oklahoma?'

"Starving!"

"That's all you were doing, starving?"

"Well, been fighting a little also."

"What do you mean fighting?'

"I fought in high school."

"OK? Well, how much do you weigh?'

"I weigh 136 pounds."

"You know you are supposed to weigh at least 145 pounds?"

"Yes, sir."

"Have you gained any weight since you have been in Texas?"

"Maybe a little. Maybe a pound, but I can gain some weight."

They continued to talk a little bit more about the job and what will be expected of him as a firefighter, and then the city manager said, "Well, Gene, we will be in touch when we have checked all of your references."

Gene immediately looking around, says, "When is the chief going to get here for the interview?"

Mr. Stiff stands and says, "I do all the interviews and hiring in the city."

Shocked, Gene got up, shook his hand, and left the office.

Can't Change Anything

Shaking his head all the way down the stairs and once outside, Gene began to wonder if he would get hired after all he said in his interview. As he drove home, he tried to run through his mind all the things he had said to the city manager. He soon parked his car in front of Betty's house, holding on to the steering wheel thinking, *did I blow my chance of becoming a firefighter.* He slowly opened the car door and walked to the house. Once Gene got inside the house, Ruby and his sister excitedly asked, "How did the interview go ... good?"

Gene said, "I met the city manager, John Stiff, nice guy, and we were talking, and I thought we were waiting for the chief who would interview me. I told him I had been fighting back in Oklahoma."

Ruby gasped. "You said what?"

"I explained it was training in high school. I didn't tell him about all the other fights I had. He also told me I should have my Texas driver's license by now. Told him we didn't have the money, but I would get it."

Ruby said, "Oh, Gene, I don't think you are going to get this job. I want you, tomorrow, to go get the driver's license."

"Wait a minute, it's worse. He said I needed to gain some weight. I need to weigh 145 pounds to get hired." With a shrug, Gene added, "Well, I can't change anything, now. We will just have to wait and see what happens after he checks my references."

"I know Bonnie at the grocery store gave you a good reference," Betty said.

"And the boss at the golf course did, too," Ruby added.

"We'll see. I still got my job in Ft. Worth. I'm thankful for that, just hate that long drive and all the money I'm spending getting there."

WAITING FOR THE CALL

The next two weeks were filled with torturous hope. On the drive each day to Ft. Worth and back, all Gene could think of was where he could find a job in Irving. The money he was spending on gas and time wasted driving was really bothering him. He and Ruby really doubted that the city was going to hire him after his interview with the city manager.

Ruby was also pushing Gene to get married. They had no time alone for the two of them and she wanted their own home. Gene, on the other hand, thought they needed to wait until he knew if he would be hired as a firefighter. Gene also knew it was a strain for Betty and Homer to have him living in the house with them and their three kids.

Finally, Gene thought it was best for him and Ruby to be married. Ruby was Church of Christ and she had found a Church of Christ pastor over by Love Field Airport who would marry them. They went and got their marriage certificate and on the next day drove over to the pastor's house to be married. Homer stood up for Gene and the pastor's wife was Ruby's witness. They said their vows and the pastor said, "Gene, you can now kiss your bride."

110 Collins Street

Gene knew he needed to buy a house and he began looking at houses after work. He would go by the fire station occasionally to see if he could find out when they were going to finish building and open the new Fire Station Two. He met a firefighter, Harold Grider, on these visits and they became friends. One day he asked Harold if he knew of a good house to buy. Harold told him that he knew of a house that was for sale and that Gene should check it out. The next evening Ruby and Gene met Harold at his house, and they drove over to look at the house for sale.

They ended up buying the house for $6,600. The owner was a military veteran, and he had a 4% interest rate on the loan that was transferable. Gene had saved $500, but the owner wanted $525 for a down payment.

Gene had met Red Whaley, the captain at Central Fire Station, and had become friends. Gene went to him and asked if he could borrow $25 for the remainder of the down payment. Whaley loaned him the $25 and told Gene he could either pay him the $25 when he got the money or work for him to pay off what he owed.

Whaley had just bought a wrecking yard on the outskirts of Irving and told Gene he could work cleaning up the place. Gene drove out to the yard, and it was a mess. It was littered with soda pop bottles, lots of soda pop bottles. He began gathering the bottles, stacking them in the front seat, back seat and trunk of his car. After a long afternoon, he drove to the convenience store and sold the bottles for over $25. Gene drove to the station and walked up the stairs to the living quarters. Opening the door and walking toward the kitchen, he saw one of the firefighters asleep on top of his bed. As he entered the kitchen, he saw one of the guys was at the table working on a crossword puzzle. Gene walked over to Whaley and handed him the $25 he owed him and said, "I have the money to pay you, plus you get my labor for the day."

"Where did you get the money?" asked Whaley.

"Sold all the soda pop bottles I cleaned up," replied Gene. Whaley and the guys all roared with laughter.

Gene still didn't have enough money to turn on the utilities for the house. He needed $20 to turn on the gas, $25 for the electricity and $15 for the water. It took him a couple of months to save up the money, but he finally got all the utilities on. And when he did, Gene and Ruby began their life as husband and wife at 110 Collins Street.

Finally, Good News!

Betty was busy cleaning up the house when the phone rang. Betty answered and found it was Chief Cronan, asking to speak with Gene Holder. She explained he wasn't home from work yet and asked if she could help him. The chief asked her to have Gene call him and that he had good news: they were going to hire him. Betty squealed when she heard the news. "Thank you, Chief Cronan, I will have him call you as soon as he gets home. Thank you again, Chief!"

Ruby, hearing the conversation from her bedroom, got up from the bed and went to the living room. After hanging up Betty turns and excitedly says, "Good news, Ruby. Gene has a job with the fire department!"

Ruby and Betty couldn't wait for Gene to get home and tell him the news. Ruby was standing by the window waiting for Gene when she saw him drive up. She ran out the front door to meet him as he opened the car door.

"Gene, you got the call from the city!" she yelled.

"Really?"

"They want you to come down to City Hall tomorrow, if you can."

"I'll be there," Gene said, thinking about how this will change the course of his life, and not knowing how true this thought would really become.

No Bridges Burned

Gene called City Hall and spoke with Chief Cronan's secretary and made an appointment for the next afternoon to meet with the chief. After tossing and turning all night, the morning finally came. Gene had been dreaming about being a real firefighter. He jumped out of bed and got ready for the drive to Ft. Worth.

In the kitchen he kissed Ruby, said goodbye to Betty and went out to his car. After turning the key to start it, he checked the gas gauge to make sure he had enough gas to make it home for the interview. On the 35-minute drive to Ft. Worth, he thought of all the money he would be saving and about the ten-minute drive he would now have to the fire station. He could hardly wait for that day.

Gene parked his car in the plant parking lot and thought, *not many more trips here.* He walked into the plant to clock in and began his day. It was hard to concentrate on his work; he was still dreaming. He was assembling the new fast action bomb bay doors on the B36 airplane. The company was retrofitting the doors of the airplane, so they would close faster after dropping an atomic bomb. The plane had to get out of there quickly before the bomb hit its target and exploded.

At lunch Gene went into his boss's office. "Sir, the City of Irving has hired me as a firefighter. I've got to give you my two-week notice. And I need to leave a little early to go talk to the chief of the fire department, if that's all right," he said.

His boss said, "I hate to lose you, Gene. You have been one of my best workers. Just clock out when you need to leave."

As they shook hands, Gene said, "Thanks for giving me the job. I really loved working on those planes."

The day wore on, but the time came for Gene to leave. He clocked out and walking to his car, he said to himself, *I've got to finish here with a job well done in case it doesn't work out with the fire department.*

Excitement That Never Left Him

When Gene got home, he took a quick shower and got ready for the interview with the chief. He drove to the fire station and pulled his car into the back parking lot. He felt extremely nervous about making a good first impression on the chief, unlike the impression he made with his interview with the city manager.

Gene took a deep breath and grabbed the doorknob to the apparatus room and entered the back door. Once inside he immediately smelled diesel exhaust from the fire engines that still lingered in the air. Walking towards the stairs, the odor of wet, smoky fire gear filled his nose, as he passed behind a fire engine. Gene began to wonder what kind of fire they had fought, a house fire, maybe a car ...

He turned and passed between the engines and saw the men's hip boots, turned down ready to be stepped into, and their wet, sooty fire coats hung on the engine's grab bars, water dripping to the floor. Gene tried to imagine himself putting on his gear and climbing on the back tailboard, holding on for dear life, to go fight fires!

He made his way up the stairs, found Chief Cronan's office and knocked on the opened door. Chief Cronan looked up and said, "You must be Gene. Come on in." He reached out his hand to shake Gene's.

They sat down and Chief Cronan asked, "Have you gained the weight needed to be hired?"

"Yes, I had to go buy some new clothes."

"Young man, all the years I've read men's applications, I never read one with that many good references and kind words about someone, especially from Bonnie."

"My dad taught us how to work. I'll do you a good job, Chief. Promise."

The chief explained what was expected of Gene for the three months of his probation period. He said Gene's starting pay would be $265 a month. Also, he would be issued a scanner for his home and would be expected to respond to all calls, day, or night. He would not receive any overtime pay for these calls. The chief told him they would make it up to him in some way. Gene didn't care. He thought *I would work for free, if I didn't have Ruby to take care of.*

"Let's go downstairs and I'll issue your fire gear," the chief said. Once downstairs, Gene got his fire coat, hip boots, helmet and heavy plastic fire gloves. By this time, the men Gene would be working with had slid the fire pole and congratulated him with firm handshakes. Gene could smell the smoke on them from the fire earlier in the day and saw that their hair was still disheveled. "We've got to pull the engines out to wash them. You want to help?" they asked Gene. The excitement of being a firefighter was building inside of Gene, and that feeling never left him his whole 56-year career.

A sad footnote to this story is Gene's sister, Betty, tragically died in a house fire later in her life. She was trapped inside the house and died of asphyxiation.

WHAT'S IN A NAME?

Legend got his name, Gene's first crew, Captain Red Whaley, Leroy Hendrix, and Harold Grider.

W hat's in a name? When someone says, "the King," you know immediately they are talking about Elvis, the King of Rock and Roll. Or if they say "Tiger," you know they are talking about Tiger Woods, the second-best golfer of all time. When someone says J Lo, they mean the pop star with the big booty. How about Air Jordan? Of course, it's MJ the GOAT of basketball. And then you have the name Shakey ... of the Irving Fire Department. This is HIS story of how he got his nickname.

Gene's mother named her son after her favorite actor and the favorite son of Oklahoma, Orvon Grover "Gene" Autry, the Singing Cowboy, who was born in the small town of Tioga, Texas, which is a part of the Sherman-Denison area where Shakey grew up. Oklahoma named a town after him: Gene Autry, Oklahoma. Autry, who appeared in 93 films, was a pioneering figure in the history of country music.

Historical Central Fire Station

So, where did the name Shakey come from? It came from the first few days of Gene's career as an Irving firefighter. He began his career at Central Fire Station on Second Street and Main. Central Station was a two-story building that also housed the city manager's office, the water, garbage, and street department, and probably the dog catcher's office. The police department, which only had one jail cell, was located downstairs. At the top of the stairs, citizens came to pay their water bill. All these offices became the living quarters for Central Fire Station when the city built a new City Hall.

On the other side of the upstairs was the living quarters for four firefighters and the fire chief's office. There was a tiny kitchen, a small bedroom and a bathroom. A living room looked out on to Second Street. The men spent most of their evenings in the apparatus room, playing pool or ping-pong. Or you could find them in the back parking lot, working on their cars, or out front, leaning back in a chair and waving at the people driving by. Wives, children, or friends would come to visit the men in these tight quarters. In the center of the bedroom, there was a fire pole to the apparatus bay. The firefighters' children loved to slide down the pole, but only with the help of the firefighters. As someone who worked at Central during my fire career, it is hard to imagine how they were able to survive in such tight living quarters—being with each other 24 hours every other day.

The Irving Fire Department has come a long way from those early years. In 2023, the City of Irving has 12 fire stations and adding a 13th on the old site of Central Fire Station. They demolished the old station but kept some of the bricks to use in the new station, preserving a part of the historical significance of Central Fire Station.

The Legend Got His Name

Gene was always kind of jittery as a kid. As a new recruit he wanted to prove himself to the men he worked with and that he could handle any situation they might encounter on any given day. He worked with Red Whaley, Harold Grider, and John Murphy, all big men that Gene wanted to impress. He wanted to show them he would be a good firefighter and he could keep his cool in any emergency.

On his third day as a firefighter, they had completed their morning duties, and all were in the small kitchen deciding what to have for lunch. Gene was standing over in the corner next to the refrigerator, trying to stay out of their way. They kept all the pots, pans, and popcorn popper on top of the refrigerator, because there was no room for them in the tiny kitchen cabinets. Being in this tight space, Gene began to get a little jittery and bumped against the refrigerator. This caused the cord to the popcorn popper to slither off and touch the back of Gene's neck. Gene immediately jumped, jarring the frig just enough to cause the stacked pots, pans and the popcorn popper to topple and tumble to the floor, and in that moment, history was made.

The other guys all got up from their chairs around the kitchen table and tried to catch the falling pots, pans and the popcorn popper. Gene thought they were trying to escape the danger so, being in the corner, he decided he needed to get out of there, quickly. "I busted out of that corner, and across the kitchen table, knocking Grider down, making it to the bedroom," Gene recalled. Once there, he was able to regain his composure and see what had really happened. He immediately began apologizing, saying, "Oh, I'm sorry, guys, I've always been a little shaky about stuff, but I'm getting better. I'll get better, I promise. I'll clean up this mess, guys!" One of the fire fighters said, "Kid, you are shaky—that's your new name, Shakey. Yep, from now on that's your name; it's Shakey!"

They got the mess cleaned up and put the pots, pans, and the popcorn popper back on top of the refrigerator. They all ate lunch, laughing at what had happened, recounting what the new rookie had done. Captain Whaley got up from the table, slid his plate in the sink, and said, "Shakey, clean the dishes and kitchen up. We will be down in the apparatus room. When you get through, come downstairs and we will train on pulling the red line. And don't ever knock over those pans again. You got it, Shakey?"

"Yes, sir," Gene replied.

The crew went downstairs and left Gene to clean up the dishes. Grider was determined to pay this kid back for knocking him down, and he had a plan. He told his captain his plan and Whaley laughed and didn't stop him. Grider went to his car trunk, opened it, and got his box out that held his paint and brushes. For the next 20 minutes, with a "steady" hand, he painted the name "Shakey" on both rear fenders of the '49 Ford.

Shakey finished cleaning the kitchen and joined his crew on the approach in the front of the station where the engine was parked. The next two hours they trained on pulling hand lines, calling him Shakey, teaching him how to pump water from the engine. Grider joins them, gives a wink and a grin to the captain, and whispered "the '49 Chevrolet has Shakey painted on both rear fenders." Whaley grinned back.

The next morning the other crew reported for duty. They were all crowded in the kitchen, drinking coffee and smoking as Grider told the guys the story of the new kid knocking all the pots, pans, and popcorn popper from atop the refrigerator. He told them about the rookie's new name, "Shakey."

Gene took the ribbing and was kind of proud they had given him a nickname. He didn't have any idea the new nickname would stick with him the rest of his life.

Best Prank Ever

Shakey had been relieved of duty and as he was leaving out the back door of the station to go home, the guys started sliding the pole to the apparatus room and running to the parking lot. Turning to see what was going on, he heard the guys yelling at him, *Shakey, look at your car, it has the name, Shakey, painted on it.* Not knowing what they were talking about, he looked towards his car and saw "Shakey" painted on the rear fender. Shaking his head, he couldn't believe they would paint his name on his car. As he rounded the back of the car, he saw the other fender was also painted, as all the guys started ribbing him about his new nickname.

"This is the best prank ever," yelled the guys. Shakey took the ribbing and finally climbed into his car. With a laugh, he drove home to show Ruby what his crew had done. Everywhere he drove his car people noticed it, and Shakey would have to tell his story. The professionally done paint job stayed on both sides of the rear fenders of his car until Shakey sold it.

The name Shakey was once again professionally painted on a vehicle he rode in all the time. Chief Knopf had "Shakey" painted over the officer door on new Engine 1 the department had ordered. It was a great tribute to a man who had devoted his life in serving the citizens of Irving, Texas, for 56 years as an Irving firefighter and to ride in it until he retired.

SUCCESS IN EVERYTHING BUT ONE THING

The question you may be asking is, *why would a man work that many years as a frontline firefighter at a busy station in south Irving?* Did he just love being a firefighter, or could there be another reason?

Shakey would often say, "I was successful in everything I did, except for one thing, my first marriage." The reality that he did get a divorce from Ruby still troubles him, today, in a deep way. "I tried my whole marriage to make her happy, but I just couldn't make her happy," he said.

In my interviews, Ruby told me that Shakey worked a lot, trying to provide for their family and she felt she was neglected. I did a little research on the divorce rate among firefighters and three studies all said the same thing. Among male firefighters the rate of divorce is 14.1% and the average for the general population among males is 16.9%. Interestingly, the rate of divorce for female firefighters is three times the rate of the national average for females. It seemed that we had a lot of divorces in our department. Because firefighters have such a close brotherhood, risking our lives and depending on each other to return to the station safe, we all felt the pain for our "brother" firefighters and their families during these divorces. Firefighters across America take care of their own because we are family.

The spouses of firefighters do have a challenging time with the 24 hours we work every third day. The schedule we work only allows us to have a normal weekend off every third week to spend with our family. Or you have the untimely emergency at home when we are at the station and our spouse must somehow manage the emergency or problem by herself. Or if there are children in the home and a problem such as a broken bone or discipline issue they must manage without their spouses' help. In the early years when Shakey and I worked, we worked an average of 56 hours a week and not for a lot of money. Almost all the firefighters had a part-time job on their days off to be able to have a better life. Shakey was one who worked a lot, working at the shopping center on his day off and late nights and weekends with his rental properties. All these factors put a huge strain on their marriage.

You Are in Big Trouble

Talk of separating for the first time began when Shakey and Ruby's kids were young and in elementary school. "I took vacation from the fire department to go to the farm to work on the house I had bought," Shakey said. "When I got home, I walked into the house and the kids were sitting on the hearth of the fireplace and Ruby told me she wanted a divorce.

She ended up leaving and moving into an apartment. Her lawyer tried to serve me with the divorce papers. They would come by the station, but they didn't know what I looked like. They would ask me if Mr. Holder was there and I would tell them that he wasn't. Or when they came to the house, I wouldn't answer the door. My brother told me to take all my money out of the bank. I told him I couldn't do that; I would be in big trouble. "You are already in big trouble," he said.

"This went on for about two or three months and one day she called and told me that her car wouldn't start. I drove over and fixed her car. She came to me and kissed me for fixing her car, and it was all over, she came back home," said Shakey.

"The next time she wanted to leave, she told me that she hated the house they were living in and wanted a divorce. So, I told her to go pick a house you like, and I will buy it. She found a house in Grand Prairie that was being built and I bought it for her. She hired a decorator and they got to pick all the colors for the house, and then we went and bought all new furniture.

"We moved in and things were still not good between us. People were telling me to sell my rental houses because the interest rates were 18%. I went to Ruby and asked her if she was going to divorce me and she told me, no, she was going to stay with me. But she still wasn't happy. I told her that when our daughter, Cindy, got married, I would give her a divorce, if she wanted one.

"No man was going to raise my kids. I would fight her the whole way until my kids are grown and out of the house."

The Third Time

Shakey began spending a lot of time away from home when he took on new responsibilities as president of the Fire Fighter's Association. Ruby was frustrated by the fact and the marriage was again in trouble. She told Shakey he was spending too much time with all those young guys and not with her. Then she said he had never done anything for her in their entire marriage.

This made Shakey mad, and he told her that all he ever did their whole marriage was for her. She repeated that he didn't do anything for her. "After this, Ruby would ask me to take her to the mall to go shopping and I would tell her I wasn't going. After a few more times of not going and buying things for her, she had had enough."

Shakey continued. "Cindy had gotten married, and I was trying to make Ruby happy, still not wanting to give up on the marriage. Ruby's sister and brother-in-law went on vacations to Florida and sometimes if I had the time, we would go with them. They were planning to go again, and I wanted to go this time and spend some time with Ruby. She didn't want to go because her family was having a family reunion at Lake Texoma the following week. I said, let's go and we could come back early so she could go to the reunion."

"So that's what we did. We went to Florida and then to the family reunion, and I had a good time at both of them, playing baseball and other stuff with her family. I thought everything was fine between us. I left the reunion on Sunday afternoon because I had to go back to work at 8 pm, because I had a half shift of vacation to use up. I drove home and got my uniform and went to work. I got to the station, and I was talking to the guys about the vacations and what a good time Ruby and I had, when the doorbell rang. My firefighter answered the door, and a warrant officer was standing there. He came into the station and I kind of knew him."

'Shakey, who in here is Gene Holder?' he asked.

"I'm Holder."

'You're not Holder,' he shot back.

"Yes, I am, Shakey Holder."

'Well, I think you made the little lady mad,' he said as he handed Shakey the divorce papers, along with a restricted order to not to have any contact with Ruby.

Don Burrows, Shakey's long-time Driver and friend said this about those years: "Shakey was lost, like a whooped puppy. He didn't know what to do. He didn't have any control over what was happening. He had left his billfold at home, so he had no cash. Didn't have his work truck; Ruby had it. It was bad for all of us, seeing our captain in that kind of situation."

Remembering that time, Shakey said, "I had a rent house that went vacant, and they left the house really dirty. They had just left, and I was in Florida, and I hadn't cleaned it yet. I had a storage unit I rented that was next to the station where I kept a bunch of my tools and stuff. That next morning, I went to the storage unit and found a pool float I could sleep on. I took some sheets from the fire station to cover up with and began staying in the rent house. I had a bunch of tools and paint equipment and lawn mowers in the storage unit that I went and sold for some cash until I got paid. I had to start all over."

What Just Happened

The divorce proceedings took two years. Ruby was paid a hefty sum for spousal support. Shakey was not really concerned about the amount money she was being paid in the beginning, thinking it wouldn't take long to settle the divorce. He also was paying lawyers' fees the whole time.

"No one was in a hurry to settle, so I finally told my lawyer he wasn't getting another dime from me, so you better get this settled," Shakey said. "Finally, the judgment came down and I asked my lawyer what had just happened. He said he didn't know."

What had happened was that the judge gave Ruby half of Shakey's pension, six of his best rent houses (she got to choose) and the 140-acre Holder family farm. Shakey was not happy that Ruby was going to get his pension. The pension plan had not clearly addressed the distribution of pension funds for the spouse in case of a divorce. Shakey believed that Ruby was not entitled to any of his pension.

An earlier divorce in the fire department set a precedent for Shakey's case, giving Ruby a pension check upon Shakey's retirement. Shakey went to the pension administrator, and she told Shakey, at the time of his retirement, Ruby would get a check from the pension fund each month, just like you. And Ruby will continue to receive a check, if you die before she does, until she dies. But if she dies before you, you will not receive what she was drawing from the pension fund. This news added to Shakey's consternation.

Shakey was really mad about the judgment. He made the statement to his men at the station, saying, "Ruby had a piece of paper that wasn't worth anything, because he would never retire."

The legend of Shakey grew once again with each passing year he worked. All of us who were working at that time wondered when he would retire. Some of us who were trying to add to our pension by adding a shift of overtime were mad when we saw Shakey had signed up on the overtime list. I asked him about it and his answer was, "I wanted to add to mine, too. I just loved working, going to the station each shift."

Did Shakey work all those years to keep his vow about Ruby not getting a dime of his retirement or did he just love being an Irving firefighter? You will have to answer that question for yourself after reading the rest of his story.

Ruby and the author after the interview.

HERDING THE CHICKENS

Shakey herding a "firefighter" at a fire.

Herding chickens is about as hard as herding cats. Cats are impossible to herd, but chickens can be trained to return to the chicken coop. You let your chickens out to roam and eat bugs and insects. While they roam, there are many dangers they could encounter, such as snakes, wild animals, and dogs. So, you must teach them with consistent patience to return to the coop, and know their boundaries. And hopefully they won't have any close calls.

Not Guilty

Several times over the course of our conversations, Shakey talked about his parenting style. "I raised my kids like chickens. I kinda just herded them, and I didn't have as much control on them as they thought I did." It was his favorite way of describing his parenting style.

One time when Shakey and I were talking about this subject, Cindy added with a slight lump in her throat, "Even my kids will tell you, the one who was most influential in their lives is my dad, their granddad. They respected their granddad."

Shakey added this to Cindy's comment: "I told all my grandkids [pointing at his boots] that if I caught them doing drugs, I'd put this pointed boot in their backsides. And please don't drink."

Shakey had seen the danger of drinking from a very young age. "Cartwright had a bunch of beer joints when I was growing up," he recalled, "and I saw a lot of drunk cowboys come across the Red River and ruin their lives. I never could see wasting my money on drinking. I would watch these men drink and be mean to their kids and wives."

"My dad shot my sister's husband, Bruce, and killed him. Bruce kept beating my sister when he got drunk, and she came home after one of the beatings. Bruce drove up from Dallas with two guns, came into the house, and told my dad to stop interfering in their business. My mother went over toward him, and he pushed my mother with the barrel of the gun, and it bruised her chest. Dad stepped in and told Bruce, 'You got the drop on us, so Betty, you need to leave and go on back home with him.'

"Dad was mad that he had hurt my mother, but he didn't want to get shot, so he let him go. You didn't mess with my mother … you were going to be in BIG trouble. So, Dad said, 'Bruce, take her home with you, but you better not ever show up here again.'

"The next evening Bruce was drinking and arguing with Betty and told her, 'I'm not afraid of that old man … he ain't telling me what I can and can't do.' Betty kept telling him he better not go back."

"He wouldn't listen and drove back up there, and my dad was ready for him. He saw Bruce pull up in front of the house, and he had his shotgun behind the chair. Bruce came up on the porch and Dad yelled, 'You can go any way you want, Bruce, but through that door.'

"Bruce opened the screen door and took two steps inside. Dad pulled the shotgun from behind the chair and shot him. It blew him out of the house and out on the porch. Mom called me at the station and told me my dad was in trouble. I asked what happened, and she replied, "Dad just shot Bruce." I replied, 'I don't have to ask if he is dead.'

"The cops came and arrested my dad and took him to Durant. They put him in a cell, but they didn't even lock it. He was there for seven days and was brought to trial. He was found not guilty by reason of self-defense. It was the fastest criminal trial in Oklahoma history. They went into the courtroom, said my brother-in-law deserved it, and set my dad free. Drinking caused a lot of problems for people. It just wasn't for me. And I didn't want my grandkids to drink either."

Allowed to Roam

Shakey allowed his three children to roam this world at a very young age, and it all started at the family farm in Oklahoma. They didn't go on many vacations. They would spend their time together roaming the bottomlands along the river with their cousins and friends. And they "sort of" knew their boundaries. This included knowing that dune buggy rides weren't always the safest thing to be doing. Over the years there were many close calls, but thankfully no one ever got seriously hurt. Shakey would let them roam and then herd them back, teaching them right from wrong. There was late-night gigging for frogs around one of the ponds. (Google it if you don't know about gigging frogs.) There were times for shooting their guns. Hunting with the coon dog's way into the early morning. Boundaries were set, and all made it out without too many scars.

Chickens at the Fire Station

Shakey also herded his "chickens" at the fire station. He set boundaries for them that he didn't want crossed, but there was freedom to roam and do it another way. Shakey said, "If you thought there was a better way, do it, but you better be right ... you better have been right."

He trained his men as he was trained, letting them have the nozzle on an interior attack. He would be right there with them, backing them up and watching how they were fighting the fire. He would correct them when they needed to be corrected, and safety was of the highest concern. They were an aggressive team, which came from Shakey's early years on the department.

He said, "A lot of officers wanted to be the one who put the fire out, but I wanted my guys to have the nozzle and get them to put the fire out, letting them have the feeling of accomplishment. It was a team effort with my driver and my two tailboards. We put a bunch of fires out."

With his years of firefighting experience, each of his many firefighters learned from one of the best, and all respected Shakey and took what he taught them to heart. His men over the decades passed on what they had learned to the next generation of Irving firefighters.

And Shakey herded all his firefighters safely back to the "chicken coop" to fight fires another day.

LARRY HOLDER

Larry fueling the '58 at Sturgis.

Firstborn children often share similar personality traits with other firstborns, and I found this to be true for me, a firstborn, and Larry Holder, Shakey's firstborn. I met Larry one afternoon at Shakey and Ginger's home with a firm handshake. He was wearing a faded Harley t-shirt and a great "biker" goatee. There was an immediate connection between the two of us. As we talked it was obvious the deep affection Larry had for his dad. Larry wanted others to know all the things his dad had done for him and how much he loved his father. He was glad we were writing his dad's story.

According to an article on the *Parents* website, "Firstborns tend to bask in their parents' presence, which may explain why they sometimes act like mini adults. They're also prone to being diligent and wanting to excel at everything they do." Sitting on the couch in Shakey and Ginger's home and listening to Larry's story, I felt this could not have been a truer statement. And most of the conversation that afternoon revolved around Larry's love for his dad and his love for motorcycles.

Dad, I Can Still Paint

I began the conversation by asking Larry, "What did you learn from your dad?" Larry replied, "Everything. I'm still learning. Dad wanted us to have better than he had, to grow up better than him. He grew up hard, learning from his dad that you had to make it on your own. He instilled that in me, and I guess in my brother and sister. I knew I had to set the example [for them]. Dad's ways used to aggravate me sometimes because he taught us by how hard he worked, and by taking us to work with him. Dad had these three rent houses. When someone moved out, I knew we were going to fix them up."

Shakey, sitting on the couch beside Larry with his arms crossed over his chest, said, "In A1 shape, like *we* were going to move into it."

"Dad would pile us [his brother and sister] into the station wagon, with paint, brushes, rollers, and all his tools. It would be a school night, and we would work till after ten o-clock. Dad taught us how to fix toilets and electrical. I can do all of that today. He was so anal about stuff ... meticulous. I would be painting a room, and he would come in and point to a spot and say, 'You got a holiday over there.' A holiday was a place where you didn't paint a small area of the wall. If it was a bigger area, it was called a vacation. I've turned out the same way; it has to be perfect."

Larry turned to his dad and said, "Dad, I can still paint. See, I have some paint on me. I'm painting my barn this week, and it is done meticulously, done right, just like you taught me."

I looked over at Shakey and said, "Shakey has some paint on his arm, too!" Shakey turned and looked at his arm and said, "I was touching up the back door and the porch post out back this morning." We all laughed as Shakey said, 'It's got to be right.'

Taught by Example

"Over the years I got my fair share of butt whooping, but he mostly taught us by example. We saw how hard he had worked, and it was so he could provide for his family. He wanted us to have fun and if there was something we liked, he would try to make it happen." Larry began to choke up and continued, "I'm trying to hold this in ... it meant so much to me to see this from dad. I've always wanted to tell him." Still striving to hold it together, he turns, hugs Shakey, and says, "Thanks, Dad. I love you."

Motorcycles and Dune Buggies

Larry declared, "My thing has always been motorcycles. It began when I was five years old. My Uncle Corky, dad's brother, bought a brand new '58 Harley. It was immaculate and I loved it. I asked my uncle if he would take me for a ride and he said, 'No, your father will.'

"Dad got on the Harley and Uncle Corky lifted me up and placed me on the chrome luggage rack behind him. 'Hold on and don't get your feet near those pipes. It will burn you,' Dad said to me as he let the clutch out and gave it some gas."

Larry leaned back and looked up at the ceiling as though he were remembering the exhilaration of riding across the Denison Dam as his dad throttled the gas, shifting gears and letting the clutch out, making those Harley pipes roar across the dam road. He declared, "That was the beginning of my love for riding motorcycles and that '58 Harley."

"When I got old enough, I asked Dad if he would buy me a minibike. He would look in the newspaper and find one to go look at. We would drive over and look at some homemade minibikes, and I would say, 'This is what I want.' But it wasn't good enough for him, and he wouldn't buy it. Me, I just wanted one, but Dad wanted the best."

"One day he told me and my brother to get in the truck. We drove to the Honda shop at Betsy Lane and Highway 183. We went in and Dad bought me and Rick each a 50cc Honda Mini Trails. Mine was red and silver, and Rick's was blue and silver. I rode the heck out of mine. This was in 1969, and Rick still has his and it still runs—and I want it, but he won't sell it to anyone."

Larry would continue to ride the minibike anywhere he could, and then he graduated to motocross racing. "I took him to his first race in Alvarado, Texas, at Paradise Valley," recalled Shakey. "As we were driving out there, I told him, 'If I like it, I'll get me one, and we will both race, but I saw him fly down into this 25-foot-deep creek. I said to myself, *I am not going to get me one and get killed on it*'. Larry won first place that day." Larry inherited his father's work ethic—he worked a paper route so he could buy more things for his motocross bike and win more races, all to make his dad proud of him.

Larry recalled when the guys at Central Fire Station began building dune buggies. "Dad went and bought a Volkswagen, and Scoop (Jimmy Cox) built our first dune buggy behind the station while they were on duty."

"That all changed when Spillman became chief," I added. Shakey agreed with a grunt. "We began racing them, but the first one wasn't fast enough; it was too heavy," Larry continued. "Dad found another one. He went and bought it and we cut most of the weight, but Dad still couldn't win the drag race. He decided to put me in the seat to race. And I won. I was only 12 and weighed less than the other guys, and this allowed me to win. Then the other firefighters began letting their son's race, but we still won. We took those buggies everywhere and raced them."

Don't Tell Your Mother!

One weekend Shakey and Larry went to their farm in Oklahoma. They called it the Ponderosa, and most of their vacations were spent there with all their cousins. There was always the usual late-night mischief happening. On this night Larry was ready to have some fun, but Shakey needed to go because he was on duty at the station the following day. Larry and Shakey loaded up the car and headed for home after dark.

When they got to Denison, Shakey pulled off the highway onto the service road outside of town. He said to Larry, "Get over here and drive." Larry looked at his dad. He was scared because he was only twelve. Shakey, seeing the look on his son's face, said, "I am about to fall asleep. You drove the dune buggies; it will be OK, get over and drive."

Larry never wanted to let his dad down and always tried to make his dad proud of him, so he got in behind the wheel. Shakey had pulled the driver's seat forward for Larry, and he sat there, gripping the steering wheel with white knuckles. Shakey walked around the car, opened the door, and slid in. "Let's go, son, and don't tell your mother."

Larry looked around at us as we sat on the couch and said, "This was a whole lot different than racing dune buggies in a field ... it was at night and with traffic. Dad turned to me and said, 'Now, just take it easy and if you need me, wake me up.' I was scared to death, but I put the car in drive, barely able to see over the steering wheel or reach the gas pedal, and off we went."

Larry recalled how he eased onto the highway and headed to Irving, trying to keep it between the lines and occasionally looking over to his dad who was sound asleep. "As we finally got into Dallas, Dad woke up and said, 'We're almost home, how you doing?'" Larry recalled. "I told him I was doing better and wasn't running off the road so often. He said he was proud of me and told me that I had learned something. Then he said to pull over and he drove the rest of the way. He reminded me not to tell my mother."

See What the Road Had for Him

A study published in the journal *Child Development* found that firstborn children are more likely to conform. They are less likely to be rebellious than second-born children, who tend to be more adventurous. In this respect, Larry didn't fit this mold of a firstborn at all. He was adventurous.

"At the age of 19, I told dad I wanted to ride to California (on his 900 Kawasaki) and visit our aunt and uncle in Los Angeles," Larry recalled. Dad said, 'Well, you always liked an adventure. Do it.' I mapped out my route, and one morning I took off with only a sleeping bag, a duffle bag, tools, and a shaving kit strapped to my bike.

"The bike didn't have a windshield, and of course there were no cell phones in those days." Dad said, as I was about to leave, 'Just call me once in a while and let me know you are all right.' Larry took a deep breath for his first trip, but not his last trip, and pulled out of the driveway to see what the road had for him.

He rode through Texas and then New Mexico and across the desert to Las Vegas. "I was too young to go to a casino but rode the Strip and across the Hoover Dam. But I didn't want to drive across the Mojave Desert in the heat, so I rested and drove across it at night," Larry said. He made it to Los Angeles, but with no cell phone for navigation, it was hard to find his aunt's house. He finally did and stayed there a couple days visiting family. It was time to head home, but not wanting to cross the desert again, he went north and found the world's largest tree, General Sherman, a sequoia tree. "The tree was massive. I never saw anything that impressive." After more adventurous riding, he made it home—sore, tired, and glad he accomplished his goal.

Hard Lesson Learned

Shakey, hearing his son reminisce about his younger days, said, "That's how my dad did it. He grew me up and didn't solve my problems, just herded me like chickens. He let me learn by myself, and I let my own kids learn early (in life). I told them that if they overdid something, they would get hurt." Larry added, "Dad had a good way of teaching, not book smart, but common sense, to think and look ahead and deal with it. We went to work early (young)." He would ask us whether we wanted to learn easy or hard and tell us that the hard lessons would stick with us.

"A good example of what I'm talking about happened one Saturday morning. I went to a friend's apartment to listen to his new stereo. My friend smoked pot and had some on the coffee table. The neighbors called the cops because we were playing the stereo too loud for a Saturday morning. There was a knock at the door; we opened it and a cop was standing there. He saw the marijuana, and we went to jail. My friend got bailed out in four hours. Dad left me there till Monday.

"A bunch of times I used the 'get out of jail free card' when I was stopped by a cop, because they all knew dad, him being a firefighter. But this time Dad was going to teach me the hard way. I was in this cell with an older Mexican man, and I was scared to death. I would give him my food, trying to make friends with him. I didn't want him to kill me during the night. He told me what would happen if I went to Dallas County, and I began to wonder where Dad was. Saturday night went, then Sunday, then Monday. They came and opened the cell, and we lined up in the hall to go to Lew Sterett [County Jail]. We get outside and I see the white bus and I'm scared. Then Robert Power (an Irving lawyer) comes over and pulls me out of the line. He said, 'You've been bailed out.' When I heard those words, I said in my heart, *there is a God.*' I added, "And his name is Shakey."

We all laughed, and Larry continued his story. "Robert Power said to me, 'Your dad is not paying me; you are, and it is $1,000. If you miss a payment, you are going to the County.' I learned the hard way this time, and I paid my debt, $100 a month and never went to jail again."

The '58

Larry wanted to tell one last story about his dad, and it involved Uncle Corky's '58 Harley. Larry owns several Harleys and enjoys long Harley trips with friends and his son. He was teaching his son the things his dad had taught him by spending time with him and letting him learn by facing the trials and tribulations these road trips bring. But Larry has never forgotten Corky's bike. "I asked my uncle several times over the years if he would sell the '58 to me, but he never would," Larry said.

"When Corky died, in his will he gave it to my cousin, Tim. Tim also rode Harleys, but I was always trying to buy it from him, but Tim wouldn't sell it to me. Unfortunately, Tim died unexpectedly, and I waited awhile and then tried to buy it from his wife, Trish. I told her I wanted the bike, but more importantly, I wanted it to stay in the family. Dad knew I was trying to buy the '58."

Shakey interrupted. "One day I called Larry and asked him, 'How much is Corky's *motor sickle* worth? Trish is wanting to sell it.' Larry said he didn't know; he would have to go and see it. So, I told him she said she had it appraised for $15,000."

Larry continued the story, saying, "I told Dad maybe it is worth that much; I haven't seen it in a long time. I don't know what shape it's in, or if it is even running. Let me ride over and look at it and see. Then Dad said, 'No need, I wrote her a check for it today.'

After a long emotional pause, Larry continued., "Dad said, 'Go get it before she changes her mind.' I kept telling my dad, 'I'll pay you for it,' and he would tell me, 'No you won't.' He said, 'I knew you wanted that *motor sickle*, and I wanted you to have it.'" Again, Larry had a quiet moment with deep emotions for his dad's love and making this dream come true.

Sturgis, No Place Like It!

"I went and got the bike from Trish and went completely through it and got it in A1 shape. In 2018 my friend Andy and I rode to Sturgis,

(South Dakota). Andy's brother, Billy, trailered his bike and the '58 up to Sturgis. I rode the '58 down Main Street and people were yelling at me, 'Great bike!' As I slowly rode past them, the whole time I was thinking of my dad and that first ride we had on it crossing the Denison Dam when I was five years old, and how my dad made my lifelong dream happen."

RICK HOLDER

Gene: noun … (informal use) a unit of heredity, which is transferred from a parent to offspring and is held to determine some
characteristic of the offspring.[3]

Planned Too Much

I drove over to Shakey's house to meet with his middle child, Rick
Holder, and to hear what he had to say about his dad. (Rick was a civil
servant like his father, Shakey, and served the citizens of Dallas with a
distinguished career as a police officer.)

I pulled up in the driveway and saw Shakey and Ginger in their garage.
As I walked up to the garage, Ginger moaned, "I probably planned too
much for today." Ginger had asked Rick and Ginger's grandson, Kagan,
to help her get her Christmas tree down from the attic.

"No problem, I'm glad to get to meet Rick," I replied.

Shakey's grandson was in the attic and handed down the Christmas
tree to Rick. Shakey yelled, "One of those totes has her ornaments. You
will just have to look through them till you find it." After a few minutes, Shakey took off up the ladder to help his grandson find the tote.

Standing on a rung of the ladder with his head in the opening, he told his grandson to look over to the left in that sack of totes. Shakey, getting impatient, finally climbed up into the attic to help with the hunt.

My firefighter training kicked in and I turned to Rick and said, "I'll climb up the ladder and make sure Shakey doesn't fall."

Rick calmly told me, "Dad is pretty stable on his feet."

"I know (remembering his name is Shakey, and he is 89), I just don't want anything to happen to him."

They finally found all that Ginger needed out of the attic, and Shakey made his way to the opening to climb down. I was there with my arm stretched out two rungs below, ready to steady Shakey as he climbed down, as taught at the Irving Fire Department drill tower. As we made our way safely down the attic stairs, he turned to me and said, "I don't need any help."

Ginger was glad that her decorations are down and said, "Why don't we go to the den and begin this interview with a cup of coffee?"

We Knew How to Work

To start the interview, I asked Rick, "Tell me what your dad taught you growing up."

"He taught me everything. First, he taught me to work hard, to have a good work ethic. Dad worked at the fire station, and on his days off he was head of the maintenance at the new Plymouth Park Shopping Center."

When it opened in 1955, Plymouth Park was one of the biggest shopping centers in the DFW metropolitan area. At 750,000 square feet of shopping space, it was a big attraction in the dawn of the mall era. It was located at Irving Boulevard and Story Road and considered the finest mall between Ft. Worth and Dallas. It was one of the first fully air-conditioned shopping centers with a wide range of businesses: Levine's, M. E. Moses, the Five and Dime Store, a toy store, jewelry store, and optometrist were some of the first tenants. Fazio's department store, Zack's Arts and Craft, and Dillard's all came in the years later.

"Dad led more by example, and when he needed help with some project at Plymouth Park, he would take me and my brother to help him. We both knew how hard he worked to provide for his family, and we knew we had to help. We used to help him put up Christmas lights ... all around that whole shopping center. We also helped Dad shoot fireworks on Ben Carpenter's ranch for the Fourth of July. We didn't really know how at first. We just learned, mostly by trial and error. We had some close calls, but nothing really happened to get someone hurt."

Shakey added, "I stopped doing it when McConachie (the assistant fire marshal for Irving) called me for some help. He shot them off for the city at the park. He was shooting them off by himself and had an accident. He had one bunch set up in a circle for the finale with a tarp over them. The wind was blowing hard, and a spark from another bunch blew over and got under the tarp, causing them all to be set off. When we got there, they said they were shooting off from all directions from under that tarp. No one got hurt, but when I saw what had happened, I said, 'Geez, this is too dangerous.' So, I stopped doing them. I was lucky all those years, but it was just not worth it."

"How much did you get paid for shooting them off?" I asked.

"I didn't get paid anything. I was on salary at Plymouth Park, and it was just part of my job. I just did what had to be done," said Shakey.

"How much did you get paid working there?"

"Oh, I got about a couple hundred a month, about the same as I got paid as a fireman."

Shakey proudly added, "Rick also went to work for Cliff Shasteen, a councilman for Irving. He was my barber, and he owned a donut shop next to the barbershop at the corner of Shady Grove and Story Road. He went to work in the donut shop all through high school ... had to get up at 3 in the morning and go to work."

I bemoaned, "Kids today haven't been taught to work, and it is a shame." Rick and his dad shook their heads in agreement.

Loved Being with My Dad

"Anything else, Rick, that your dad taught you?"

"Yes, Dad also would say, 'Sometimes it is not *what you do*, but *what you don't do*.' What he meant was, don't do things that will get you in trouble that will follow you the rest of your life."

"You were a Police Officer, for Dallas, weren't you?" I asked.

"Yes, for 35 years. I retired five years after my dad retired."

I marveled, "That is incredible, and it just emphasizes the long career your dad had. I bet you saw a lot of young people in your 35 years do something stupid that followed them all their life?"

"Yes, unfortunately."

I nodded in agreement and said, "What else do you remember about being Shakey's son?"

"One thing that wasn't helpful was when I had trouble with my car, I would drive it to the station. I would go in and tell Dad, 'Something is wrong with the car.' He and all his men would come out to see what was wrong. One would pop the hood and start it up to listen to it. I would stick my head under the hood with them, not having a clue what was wrong or how to fix it. One of the guys would go get his tools out of his truck. Another would give me a dime for the Coke machine, and I would go inside and drink a Coke—while *they* fixed my car. What was unfortunate is that to this day, I don't know how to fix anything on my car! The guys at the station always fixed it for me."

"What I did love was spending time with my dad at the station. He was gone so much of the time working at Plymouth Park or on his rent houses, I didn't get to see him a lot of the time, so spending time with him at the station was great. Anytime I could, me and my friends would go to the station and hang out. My friends wanted to see them get a run and watch them leave. Me, I just wanted the time with my dad. The guys at the station were like family to us. We went on vacation with them, raced our dune buggies, and went to the farm. It was great."

Kid Was Just Stupid

"Any funny stories about your dad?" I asked.

"Well … don't know if I should tell this one, but me and my buddies would come to the station at night and hang out and shoot pool. Dad had this new rookie, and he was a bully. He came over and started picking on me and my friends and put one of them in a headlock. Dad came in and asked what was going on. The rookie said, 'I'm picking on them and will pick on you, too.'

"Dad went over to him and challenged him, 'Just try to pick on me.' The rookie made a fatal mistake and challenged him. Dad grabbed him and picked him up and threw him under the pool table. He told him not to get out until he told him he could get out, and the kid stayed there until me and my friends left."

Shakey added, "The kid was just stupid and always causing trouble. One day we were out in the apparatus room doing something, and he just could not stop from doing something stupid. I had enough of his bull and grabbed him and threw him inside the bathroom out there in the apparatus room, but while I struggled getting him in there, my shoe came off inside the bathroom. The other firefighters went and got a bed slat, and I tied the door shut with it. It was a real hot summer day, and the chief showed up. I met him in the apparatus bay and we talked for a bit. Then the chief saw the door tied up with the slat and asked, "Why is that door tied up?" I replied that I didn't know why.

"The chief told me to open it, so I did. The kid was lying on the floor sweating, and water came running out of there. He had thrown my shoe in the toilet and flushed it, stopping it up. I told the chief, 'If I knew he was in there, I would have let him out.'"

"The Chief just left, shaking his head, knowing that was *my* shoe in the toilet. The kid finally got fired; he couldn't pass any of the tests they gave him."

"That is too funny, Shakey," I said, as Ginger and Rick nodded in agreement.

Shakey, thinking back on his career, said, "As a firefighter and being at work for 24 hours, there is a lot of time to pull pranks, and on rare occasions a fight would happen. I loved every minute of it."

Final Thought

These were Rick's last words about his dad. "The thing about Dad is, he is a people person. Dad is just a good guy. He took care of a lot of people and good people wanted to be around him. Even when I was a teenager, I enjoyed hanging out with him. Dad is fond of telling the story about buying my first car. The first night I had it, as I drove off with my friends, he reminded me to be careful. We weren't gone long. When I walked in the house, Dad was surprised that I was already back. He asked, 'What are you doing home so early.' I responded, 'Just thought I would come home and agitate you.' We spent the rest of the evening together, watching TV. He is a great dad to have. To this day, I still enjoy spending time with him!"

CINDY HOLDER JEFFERY

Cindy with her dad.

At a very young age, Cindy began to love the Irving Fire Department, and she was always a "daddy's girl." When she was growing up, her dad worked a 24-hour-on and 48-off schedule, and he was working at his part-time job at the shopping center. Plus, his rent houses kept him busy. Somehow Shakey found time to spend quality time with Cindy and her brothers, teaching them what was important in life, their family and friends and helping others.

When Shakey was at the fire station, Cindy and her brothers would be on their bellies on the living room floor, waiting to hear their dad be dispatched to an emergency, wanting to know what kind of emergency it would be.

Shakey commented, "She listened to that scanner from the time she was born."

Cindy recounted, "The scanner had a bulb in the top of the box and when it turned green, we knew dad might be going on a fire call. It was so exciting to me to hear my dad going to help someone."

Always a Firefighter

"There were times when I would be going somewhere with Dad, and he would see an accident or fire. Once we went somewhere and saw a fire. Dad pulled over to the side of the road and stopped. As he was jumping out, he turned and said, 'I'm going to help; don't get out of the truck and I'll be right back.'" And off he would go, and Cindy would watch all the heroic actions of her dad. "Dad was always happy being a firefighter," Cindy said with a big smile.

Once, as Cindy and Shakey were going to a dune buggy race, they drove up on a one-car accident. Ronnie Mayo was following them, pulling his dune buggy. Shakey and Ronnie both got out to help. Cindy could see from her seat inside their truck that the car was badly damaged.

She said, "Dad and Ronnie tried to open the door, but it was too badly damaged. They kept trying to get the driver out when I heard sirens. The fire department was close by and got there quickly and were able to get her out. Unfortunately, she died, but watching Dad trying to help made me very proud."

Shakey said, "Ronnie and I had another accident a week earlier in Euless. It was raining really hard, and the sixteen-year-old driver lost control and slammed into a light pole. Her brother's face hit the windshield. There was blood everywhere. This was the third accident Ronnie, and I came up on and when we got back into the truck—soaking wet—Ronnie said, "I'm going to quit running around with you. You are just bad luck."

Favorite Firefighter

Cindy, remembering all the firemen that dad hung out with and how they became like family, said, "They would be over to the house all the time, or going to the farm, or dune buggy racing with Ronnie and his family and Jimmy Cox. It was great times."

Bear Bryant was one of her favorites. She and her brothers would agitate him when they went to the station. "I was six or seven years old, and we were at the farm in Oklahoma. Bear always was chewing tobacco, but I thought it was a brownie! He offered my brother, Ricky, and me a bite of his "brownie" one day. I loved brownies and he cut us a piece off and handed it to us. I put it in my mouth and chewed it a couple of times, and we both ran to the water hose, spitting and gagging all the way. Bear just roared with laughter loving every minute of it."

Shakey said, "Me and Ronnie became good friends, but not at first. (You will find out more in Ronnie's story.) He came to work for me when I was at Two's, and it started off bad as soon as he walked into the station. I told him, if you do your job, you'll think I'm the greatest guy on this fire department. If you don't, you ain't going to be on my ass cause you ain't going to be here."

Ronnie had retired before Shakey retired, and when the department was having Shakey's 50th anniversary party, Ronnie told him he wasn't coming. Shakey told him, "You are coming, and I'm going to kiss you right in the mouth." Ronnie did show up at the party, and when he walked to the podium, Ronnie kissed Shakey. It was a deep brotherhood because of all the close calls they had serving the citizens of Irving.

Working at a Young Age

Cindy, like her brothers, learned to work at a young age. She recalls pulling weeds at the rent houses and cleaning or painting rent houses late at night. When she was six years old, she mowed the grass at one of the rent houses. "I was pushing the lawn mower, and I could barely see over the handle. It was 100 degrees, and I was complaining to Dad, saying, 'Dad, I'm so hot I'm going to throw up.' All he said to me, 'When we get finished, I'll buy you a hamburger and Coke.' And he did!"

"Dad taught us how to work. Sometimes when Dad was working at Plymouth Park Shopping Center, he would take me with him and leave me in the office to answer the phone while he worked."

Shakey added, "She got a job when she was 12 at the Village Inn Restaurant across from Texas Stadium on the service road, washing dishes."

Cindy, rolling her eyes, said, "Dad, I wasn't 12."

"Yes, you were, and after a few weeks, they needed a waitress because they were shorthanded and had a game at Texas Stadium. They gave her this waitress dress, and we still have it."

Cindy said, "I do remember that. I was so nervous. I poured this guy a cup of coffee and I bumped the cup, spilling the hot coffee in his lap. I started apologizing and he said it was okay. And then he gave me a $36 tip. When I told Dad, he said, 'You better do that again if they give that big of tips.'

"I loved working at Plymouth Park Baptist Church when I was in high school. It was a school program, and I helped teach the little kids."

"She would take them to the zoo on the weekends," Shakey said. "You couldn't do that today, but back then you could. All my kids worked and had jobs at an early age."

Help Me Get These Kids Out of My Car

Shakey made time for all his children and wanted them to have fun. This included Cindy and her girlfriends. She was in sorority in high school, and they had a fundraiser at the old Texas Rangers Ballpark. Shakey loaded up the station wagon with all the supplies they needed and drove them out to the stadium. After a long day they headed home, and the girls asked Shakey to drive them by Gibson's Discount Store to see what boys were hanging out in the parking lot. They told him not to stop, just drive through.

Cindy said, "We didn't want any boys to see us with my dad." Then they asked him to drive to the library (across from Irving High School). They didn't want him to pull up to the library because it was one way in and one way out. It was "stop and go" traffic as people were talking to each other.

"I wanted to have some fun and I pulled into the library and the girls began screaming and looking for blankets to cover up," recalled Shakey. "I was having to wait for the traffic to move and saw a group of boys. I rolled down the window, and the girls started yelling at me to stop, and I yelled, 'Hey, boys, come over here for a minute.' About five boys came over and I said, 'I picked these girls up from down the street and they won't get out. Will you all help me get them out of here?'"

Cindy said, "We were totally mortified. Dad did everything with me and my girlfriends and they still love him like their own to this day."

Shakey echoed the love, saying, "I had just as much fun as they did."

Homesick

Cindy graduated from Irving High School, and Shakey wanted her to get a college education so she could get a good job and provide for herself. Cindy really wasn't ready to leave to go to college. Shakey was in the middle of his divorce with Ruby, and Cindy felt she needed to be home with her dad. They finally decided she would go to North Texas University in Denton, Texas. Shakey said, "It was close to home, and I paid her tuition and bought her a new car."

The day came to go to college, and Cindy loaded everything possible into the car and drove to Denton. She hated it as soon as she got there, making every excuse she could to come home. Shakey kept telling her she couldn't come home. She called him all the time to tell him she was coming home. "It was horrible, and I cried constantly. I would have to stretch the phone cord into the closet because I cried so much, and my roommates couldn't study or hear the television."

One night, she called her dad again from the closet, crying and telling him again that she wanted to come home. Shakey emphasized the fact he had paid the tuition, and she would have to finish the semester and then if she still didn't like it, she could come home. Cindy had had enough, and two hours later, with all her belongings in the car, she walked into their house.

With red swollen eyes, she said, "How long are you going to be mad at me?"

Shakey replied, "Only for about 15 minutes."

Shakey Got What He Wanted

Her dad still wanted her to get an education. With a lot of discussion between the two of them, Cindy found the Executive Secretarial School and enrolled. It was a ten-month extensive preparation for the business world.

Shakey mused, "It cost me more for her to go to that ten-month school than it did for Rick's four-year college education."

After graduation, the school found her a career with a prestigious law firm in downtown Dallas. She has had a successful career for 42 years with the law firm.

"Dad taught me how to work, to be honest, to be loyal, to always look to help the underdog, and to be kind to everyone you can."

Shakey said, "You will never regret being kind; it doesn't cost you a thing to be kind. If you say bad things to a person, you will go home and regret it. Just be kind."

Herding My Chick

"One time Dad and I visited a friend of his from Oklahoma that he helped occasionally. He wanted me to see how some people choose to live."

Shakey said, "The man was an alcoholic, didn't have a relationship with his parents, and married this good-looking woman and they had five kids. They lived in a filthy trailer that sat on a bed of dirt just beside the road. Because all of his money went to alcohol, the family really didn't have much at all. This particular summer day, the kids weren't allowed to go inside the trailer, hadn't eaten, and had no shoes on. I got them something to eat and gave them some money ... all of which most likely was spent on liquor."

Cindy said, "We talked about the family all the way home. I told Dad, 'I felt sorry for the kids and would run away from home if I had to live like that. Dad told me, 'No, you wouldn't. You wouldn't know any better.'"

"I just wanted her to see how other people lived."

This simple act had a tremendous effect on Cindy, and she remembers it vividly to this day. She recalls, "The lesson I learned that day ... be extremely thankful for the caring, hardworking, generous and stable father I called Dad."

Rent Houses

Cindy is not only working for the law firm, but she is also managing the rental property that her dad owns. Cindy knows how generous her dad has been with these tenants.

Cindy stated, "Dad is the best landlord ever! Over the years he has let too many to count to live for free. A lot took advantage of his compassion. He wouldn't evict them when they hadn't paid their rent if they were having hard times."

Shakey said, "One woman rented from me for six years and lived for free for over two years. Years later the mother of the woman called and thanked me for what I did for her daughter. She told me she was now doing good in life."

My interview ended that day with Shakey saying, "Always be generous ... always be generous and kind, helping others be the best they could be, working hard, love having fun with my kids and their friends, herding the chickens, and having a loving daughter, during the good times and the bad."

WHAT YOU SEE IS WHAT YOU GET

On a beautiful June morning in Shakey's backyard around an umbrella table, Ginger introduced me to Margie, Shakey's younger sister. Shakey soon joined us, sweating from working in his yard. In the swimming pool was Shakey's great grandson, Jaxon, swimming and having a big time.

As we introduced ourselves, I found out that Margie was still working. She told me she has worked longer than her brother. She is 87 years old and still working part-time, five days a week?? She's even been asked by her manager to climb a ladder to reach something high on a shelf over her much younger co-worker. Much like her brother, her upbringing has served her well.

Problem Solver

"Margie, what do you think of your brother?" I asked.

With a sparkle in her eye she says, "Huh, like everyone else thinks of him. He was born that way; all of his life he has taken care of all of us. We had a very good father, but we had Gene."

"And he is not the oldest?"

"That's right! Every one of us has relied on his judgment, his advice, and his confidence in us. And we knew what he expected from us."

Ginger jumped in and said, "He once fixed your shoes one time."

Margie giggled, remembering the circumstances, "Gene was maybe six and I was four, and each of us only owned one pair of shoes. It was like a ballerina shoe with no sole. Once he got my shoes and wore them in the mud and left them wet and muddy. I got up the next morning and found them muddy and the bottom cracked."

Shakey said, "She had worn out the sole. I found a piece of cardboard and cut it to fit inside the shoe and would fix them. It worked until we got them wet, and I would put some more cardboard in them."

Margie said, "We grew up poor, but we had a wonderful, wonderful family."

Shakey nodding in agreement said, "You didn't mind going home. We always managed to have a warm blanket in the winter and sheets in the summer."

"We had good parents. Mother always expected us to be something; we couldn't be white trash or poor. She would tell us we were better than that," Margie proudly said as she looked at Shakey nodding in agreement.

"Our parents didn't solve our problems. You had to solve your problems yourself," Shakey added.

"Truthfully, we gave all our problems to Gene. When we were young and when we were old ... we still go to him, and my children go to him for advice. He's always been there ... and he would tell it like it is. Maybe not what you wanted to hear, but he would give us his advice. We all knew, if he tells you, he's telling you the truth," said Margie.

Mass Grave

"Once when we were little kids, Gene stepped in a red ant bed and killed an ant. There was a little kid playing with us, real sensitive kid, and he saw Gene had killed the ant and told him he had to bury it. Gene puffed up and told him, 'Who cares about a red ant?'

Then Gene went in there and stomped the bed of ants killing a bunch of them. The little kid said, 'Now, you are going to have to bury all of them.' Gene assured him he was not going to bury those red ants. The little kid, on the verge of tears, says, 'Oh, come on, bury those red ants.' Gene began digging a big hole and started to rake the ants into the hole, and the little kid protested, 'You have to bury each ant in his own hole.' Gene said to him, 'That ain't going to happen.'"

Shakey adds, "I was probably six and Margie hadn't started school and she begged me to bury them, but they were in a mass grave, as the little kid was standing there crying, wanting me to bury them individually."

Paint is Cheap

Margie continued to talk about her brother and said, "This is another brother thing. I was living in Florida when my husband died. I decided I needed to move back to Irving and found a house and bought it. Now, I had never paid a bill in my whole entire life. Never, ever fooled with nothing!

"So, I wanted to paint my house and went to the paint store in Plymouth Park. I got what I needed and went home and painted the house by myself. When I finished, it was bleeding through, and I was so upset. I had Gene come over to take a look at it. When he got there, I'm crying and I told him, 'I painted all this and look at it.'

"Without compassion, Gene says, 'Paint is cheap. Paint it again.' So, I got myself up and drove back down to the paint store and I told them, 'I need more paint, and charge it to my brother; charge all of it to my brother.' Later, when I saw him again, I said, 'Paint was cheap, wasn't it?'"

Reflecting, Margie said, "I thought my brother would show me some sympathy, would feel sorry for me, and solve my problem. All I could hear him say is '*Paint is cheap, paint it again.*' Gene always said if you can solve it with money, you ain't got a problem."

"When Margie called me from Florida and told me Ben just died, I told her, 'You got a problem.' Money couldn't solve that," said Shakey.

Margie continued, "But when I called him and told him Ben had died, I never picked up the phone again ... because he would take care of it ... never thought about doing absolutely nothing else." Margie paused for a second to think and said, "To tell you the truth, I don't even remember driving back to Texas. I knew Gene would solve my problem like he always had."

A Big Problem

"She was nearly that bad when her second husband, Lee, died," Shakey said.

"I had a big problem," Margie said. "Lee was Jewish. And I had called other funeral homes and they told me they had to do it their way. I told them my side was not Jewish, so we have to compromise.

"They kept saying, 'Nope.' So, I said to myself *I don't know what to do.* I went to Gene and told him the problem.

"He said, "Let's go see Genie at Ben Brown [Funeral Home]."

"So, we went down there and they were extra nice, because they knew Gene."

Shakey quipped, "I used to tell Genie all the time that Ben said he would bury me for free. And she would say, he never told me that."

Superman Strength

Shakey spent his entire adult life with the Irving Fire Department risking his life, saving people who were in dangerous situations, and fighting fire with primitive equipment and fire gear. But this heroism began at a very young age. We ended that morning with Margie recounting the day Shakey rescued their sister.

"Me and my older sister, Betty, and Gene were walking across this narrow bridge after a big rain. We were crossing the bridge and Betty bent over for some reason and fell in. The water was about a foot from the bottom of the bridge and really swift. Gene immediately reached down and grabbed her arm as she was holding on to the bridge. The water was really swift."

Shakey said, "If I hadn't have grabbed her when I did, we would never have gotten her out. Under that bridge was a bunch of bushes and limbs and barbed wire."

Margie said, "I will never forget this because she was gone. Her head had gone under water. He had Superman strength to pull her out—and saved her life."

World Will Seem Easy

Shakey, listening to this story, turned to me, and said, "I told you already about Dad saying, 'When I turn you loose, the whole world will seem easy.' And it seemed easy for me, to earn a living, to raise kids. And everyone who I worked with and met has had an influence on me as much as I had an influence on them. I never put a fire out by myself. I always had help, and I listened to them."

Margie added, "One day I drove by a large apartment fire and saw all this fire. Next time I saw Gene, I asked, 'How on earth do you pull up on a big fire and put it out?' He told me, 'I never went to a fire that I thought I couldn't put it out.'"

"I knew I got paid to put fire out," Shakey replied.

And that is what Shakey did. *A job well done!*

I'M GOING TO CHANGE YOUR LIFE

Finally a wedding. Finally married.

One Saturday morning, Shakey was sitting at the kitchen table at the fire station and said to Don Burrows, his long-time driver, "I've been a nice guy all my life. But the women I seem to meet think only of themselves. Geez, I don't want to be with a woman like that." Don wisely replied "Shakey, don't give up, one day you will meet the right woman."

I drove to McKinney, anxious to finally interview Ginger and hear her story about being married to Shakey. I pulled into their driveway, and Ginger and Shakey were sitting on their porch in their white rocking chairs while the sprinklers were watering their lawn. We greeted each other and Shakey asked me to have a seat. He immediately starts telling me new stories about his life. And I have another good laugh hearing him recall people he had met or worked with and their stories. After a bit, I said, "Let's go in. I want to hear all about this love story."

Shakey replies, "Y'all go on in; I want Ginger to tell the story and read what she says in the book."

Meeting Shakey

Ginger and I go into their breakfast nook and take a seat at the table. I asked her, "How did this love story begin?"

"I guess I will start when I was driving with my mom to go to my house that was way off in the country. My divorce was not yet final, but she was helping me get my house ready to sell. And on the way there, I got a speeding ticket. I didn't want to pay for it, so I took that driver's ed class. So, I went to the class and one of my daughter's good friends, Carol, worked there. After this we became friends.

She knew I had gotten a divorce, and one day she said, 'I want you to come with me and my boyfriend and go meet someone.' I immediately said, 'No, I'm not ready to meet anyone.' She kept insisting saying, 'You got to do something.' She bugged me for weeks, so one night she called and said, 'We're going to Oklahoma, and we want you to go and meet our friend who will meet us there. I finally agreed to go, and they said they would come over and pick me up.

" I was real nervous while I got myself ready. Carol and her boyfriend came and picked me up and we drove to Oklahoma. While we were driving, she was telling me all about this guy I was going to meet, and I got even more nervous. We got to the bar, and the guy I was supposed to meet never showed up. "Carol was so upset, and her boyfriend said, 'Let's go to this other place and have a good time.' I wasn't sure now what to do or say, but again finally said OK. We went to the other bar, still in Oklahoma, and I'm sitting there looking around while Carol and her boyfriend are dancing. I kept noticing this one guy staring right at me. I said to myself, *why is he staring at me*?"

Ginger, thinking back on that night, giggled, and continued, "I finally turned around and saw this large screen TV with a rodeo on ... that he was watching. He wasn't looking at me; he was watching a rodeo. I was so relieved and now ready to go home."

"They finished their dance and Carol came to the table, and I told her about the guy staring at me. Then her boyfriend came to the table and sat down, reached, and squeezed my leg under the table. He turned out not to be a very good guy, but I immediately jumped when he grabbed me. My friend knew what had happened, and she got really mad at him."

"She sent him to go pay the bar bill, and this other guy came to our table. He asked Carol to dance. She is really a cute girl, but she yelled, 'Hell no, I don't want to dance. I don't want to do nothing.' "The guy replied, 'I didn't want to either, but my brother wants to meet your friend.'" Ginger paused, thinking back on this life-changing night and says, "This guy was Dale, Shakey's brother. My friend was still really mad at her boyfriend but yelled over the music, 'Tell him to come on over.'

"So, Dale went and got Shakey. They both came over to the table and the first thing Shakey ever said to me was, 'If you are married, and you want me to, I will kill him.' My divorce was not yet final, but I thought ... *I would like this guy to…*" Ginger said, laughing at the thought and not finishing the sentence. "So, this man got my immediate attention."

The Date

Ginger continued, "Shakey then said, 'I would like to go out with you. Can I have your number?' I really didn't know about bars and dating stuff, so I pressed him to give me his number. I told him I would call him. Shakey said, 'No, you will never call.' He kept pressing me and finally talked me in to giving him my number. When I gave him my number, I thought, *gosh, he might be a rapist or something.* I then remembered he had told me he was a firefighter and I thought, *He's probably a good guy.*

"Driving home with my friend, I told Carol, "The guy we met, his name was Shakey, and I have given him my number." And she shot back, 'Don't matter, they never call ya', still fuming about how the night was ending. I said, "OK, that's good," but the next day Shakey did call me. When I heard his voice, I thought, *oh my goodness, he did call.* That's when he told me, 'I'm going to change your life.'"

"We talked a bit and then he asked if we could go out to dinner and I told him, OK. But I told him where I wanted to go. It was a place where my son's best friend, Garth, worked. I knew I would feel like I had some protection going to this restaurant."

"The night came, and we went to the restaurant. Shakey was great and the date went great. He got along with Garth and everyone else at the restaurant. I started thinking, *this guy is really nice.* I then got the surprise of my life! He said, 'I'm going to marry you.' I said, 'Oh my gosh! Are you crazy? You must be lonesome.' He shot back, 'I'm *not* lonesome.' He was dating other women. I think he must have shooed them off, because he was seeing me now all the time."

"Shakey didn't give up on trying to get married. So, I shooed him off a couple of times and tried to make him forget me. After this he began sending me roses all the time where I worked at the elementary school. The first time he sent me flowers, they were beautiful, three dozen roses. They were so beautiful that my sister made me an artificial arrangement just like the one Shakey gave me. They are still at the top of my stairs, so I can remember that day."

"While we were dating, he would always bring up Ruby, and at the same time my daughter was giving me a lot of trouble. I told him, I think maybe we should stop dating. He didn't like it that I said this. He backed off for a while, but when he did call, I was ready for him to call."

"We dated for three years. I was like, *OK, guy, let's do this. We can't date forever.* My principal even said to me, 'He has given you all kinds of rings. When is he going to give you the right kind of ring?' He even bought me a car, a nice Mustang. One night I got down on my knees and said, "Let's get married." I was thinking, *Dang, I'm already close to fifty, I can't wait much longer.* He kept dragging his feet, and I thought maybe I need to date someone else. This other guy, David, had been calling me and I decided to go on a date with him."

It Almost Ended

"I had called in sick to the school with pink eye, and David came over to my house to see me. We were talking, and I saw Shakey drive up. I immediately said, 'I'm in trouble. My boyfriend just drove up. Go hide in the closet.' But instead, he went into the hall bathroom. Shakey knew how to get into the house, so I ran upstairs and jumped in my bed with all my clothes on. Shakey got in and called out and I told him I was in bed. He came up and told me he wanted us to go see Julie's (Ginger's daughter) new baby. I protested that I couldn't with pink eye. I didn't need to be around the baby. But he insisted. So, I got out of bed, with my clothes on, and we went downstairs."

When we got to the bottom of the stairs, Shakey opened the bathroom door where David was. They had a stare-off, and I'm thinking the whole time, *this is going to be bad.* Shakey finally says, 'What are you doing in there?' David said, 'Everyone has to be somewhere.'"

"Shakey was really hurt. We had been in a great three-year relationship. David was interested in me, but I wasn't interested in him. I was hoping this would spur Shakey to marry me."

"Shakey walked out the front door and I followed him, pleading for him to stop and talk. He got into his truck, and I was crying, trying to get him to stop and talk to me. I asked him about us going to the big Valentine dance party we were supposed to go to the next week. He finally said, 'I don't know.'

"As I watched him drive off, I said to myself, *well, this is over*. I went into my house crying and called Jean, my best friend, and told her what had happened. She and I talked for a long time. I finally told her, 'I'll go sit on his doorstep, until he takes me back.'"

A Once in a Lifetime Valentine Party

Valentine's day came and Ginger didn't know for sure if Shakey was going to come pick her up, but she got ready just in case. Soon, Shakey called and told her he was coming by to pick her up for the party and Ginger was relieved and happy. She went to her window waiting for him to drive up and soon he pulled into the driveway. He came to the door and Ginger gave him a kiss and they drove to Texas Stadium, still not sure if everything was alright between them.

Once inside the ballroom, Ginger looked around at the huge crowd that had gathered for the party. Chief Knopf yelled, "Over here Shakey!" and Ginger and Shakey went and sat down at their table. After they had enjoyed a wonderful meal, they were sitting around the table talking to the Knopf's, as Ginger hoped that everything between the two of them was now behind them.

The emcee got up and thanked everyone for coming and hoped they had had a good time. After a few more comments he asked, "Is there anyone else who wants to say something before we end this wonderful evening."

Shakey stood up and grabbed Ginger's hand without saying a word. Ginger was now being pulled to the stage and as they were climbing the steps to the platform, she wondered *what is going on*. The emcee handed Shakey the microphone and he got down on his knee and looking up at Ginger proposed to her. The crowd broke out in shouts of congratulations and all Ginger could do was stare at the ring on her finger and then give Shakey a big kiss.

Shakey told me in one of our interviews, "The reason I proposed the way I did, in front of all those people, was I knew she couldn't say, no."

Finally, a Wedding

I asked Ginger to tell me about their wedding. "Well, it was getting out of hand. Shakey, being good friends with Chief Knopf and going on many vacations with him and his wife, thought we should have a big wedding. He talked about having the ceremony in the snorkel basket on Truck Two. It just kept getting bigger and bigger. Shakey and I finally decided enough of this.

"We drove to my sister's house in Mississippi and eloped. We found out we had to go to the courthouse and the judge explained everything to us. He told us we had to wait to see if I was pregnant or not, or something like that. We laughed because of our age. So, he gave us a waiver, but he said, 'If I give this waiver, you got to promise you will never get a divorce.' Shakey and I looked at each other and just laughed.

"My sister, Carolyn, planned a small wedding at her house. She told our parents to come over to the house and wear some nice clothes. She told them we were going to take some pictures. She arranged for the justice of the peace to come over to do the service. This guy had just become the justice of the peace and was really nervous. He knew my sister and brother-in-law were big socialites in town, and he was shaking more than me and Shakey.

"My parents showed up and were shocked that we were getting married. My dad knew that Shakey was part Indian and called him Blanket and asked, 'Where are my ponies?'" Ginger said with a laugh, "He was wanting his dowry. We had some of my nieces there, but not Cindy, Shakey's daughter, or my daughter, Julie. They have never forgiven me to this day for not being invited. Shakey's boys didn't care, but the girls were hurt."

The Honeymoon

"We went on our honeymoon with my parents. We had gone on many vacations with them in the past. It was always funny to me and Shakey that they wouldn't let us sleep together when we went with them, with me being close to fifty years old and dating that long. Every time we went together, I would stay with my mom, and Shakey and Dad shared a room. We drove to my mom's brother's place on the coast for our honeymoon. Mom and Dad stayed at her brother's, and Shakey and I stayed with a first cousin in her house. The next morning Mom calls me, but Shakey answers the phone. When he heard her voice he said, 'Mazie, I want to tell you, me and your daughter consummated our marriage last night.'" Ginger laughing, thinking back to that morning said, "My mother yelled, 'Let me talk to my daughter.' It was crazy, but we were finally married."

"Later we went on another honeymoon with the Knopf's to Cancun. It was a good time. And I still remember that first date, when he said he would change my life. And he did!"

Ginger's Final Words from Her Heart

"He was a really good boyfriend, but he is an amazing husband for me. He loves me with a love that I never had before or since.

"He gave me three more children, and they are the best kids anyone could ever have! Larry, Rick, and Cindy, I love you.

"He became the stepdad for my two children, Will and Julie. He is an amazing dad to them, also the granddad to my two grandchildren, Kagan and Amanda. They know no other 'Granddad.' He also has one great grandson, Jaxon. To them he is Superman!

"He also gave me my dream house. I call it our Mississippi house in Texas.

"He was also my Teacher's Aide for my school classes. He always would do my bulletin boards and decorate my rooms.

"He took me to many places I would never have been able to see, including many states in the U.S. and many countries abroad. Times I will never forget. When we traveled, Shakey made everything fun!

"He loved my family, my mom and dad and sisters and brother. He loved and respected them. They loved him as much as they loved me.

"He not only changed my life, he made life so much better. All our 35 years together have not been without some bumps. As Don Burrows, said, 'Shakey can be as stubborn as a goat.' But Shakey is my GOAT, Greatest Of All Time!

"Shakey, you are my HERO!!!" concluded Ginger.

THE TRUCK

Shakey's 1989 Chevy half-ton

S hakey has been very generous about buying cars for his family. For Larry's sixteenth birthday, Shakey bought him a 1967 El Camino. "After a year, Larry tore it apart with some friends to make a show car out of it. They took the motor out and stripped the paint off the car and never finished it and just left the car at my friend's garage," Shakey recounted. "I was mad and went and told the garage to put it back together and then sold it for less than it cost me to fix it. Larry wanted me to buy him another, but I bought him a motorcycle instead. Ruby made me buy him a car when he graduated."

"When it was time to buy Rick a car, he would find one he wanted and ride his bike over there and look at it when I was at work. Once he rode all the way to Haltom City to look at a car. I finally bought him a used Firebird and then when he went off to college, bought him a new car and gave the Firebird to Cindy. She drove that in high school and when she went off to North Texas [University] I bought her a Camaro.

You know what, when I sold the Firebird, I sold it for $2,000 more than I paid for it."

He bought Ruby several cars during their marriage, bought his mom a couple of cars, and his younger brothers all drove cars Shakey bought for them. Soon after Shakey started dating Ginger, he bought her a nice Mustang convertible. Shakey has bought Julie, Ginger's daughter, several cars. Robby, Ginger's son, once asked Shakey to buy him a car. At this point in life Robby had been a little rebellious. He had grown his hair to the middle of his back and Shakey was not fond of it, to say the least. Robby called and asked Shakey if he would buy him a car.

"I will if you get a haircut," replied Shakey.

"What is wrong with my long hair, didn't Jesus have long hair?" asked Robby.

"And Jesus walked everywhere he went," said Shakey. He did end up buying Robby a car, after he cut his hair.

I finally asked Shakey, "Why did you buy your family all these cars?"

"Because they were all poor," he shot back.

"Shakey probably can't think of all the cars he has bought," Ginger replied. "He just really cares for people."

Shakey always drove trucks. When he worked for Plymouth Park Shopping Center, they provided him with a work truck that he drove for years. And, when the owners sold the shopping center, they gave him the truck. It was worn out, but Shakey gladly accepted it and used it for a work truck for his rent houses. However, Shakey somehow lost the truck when Ruby was awarded it in the divorce decree. Shakey decided he needed to go buy a new truck. Unfortunately, he wrecked it shortly after he purchased it.

On a rainy day, he was driving too fast down Beltline Road and hydro-planed. The truck began to spin and went up over the curb taking out some light poles. The Fire Department responded and after checking to make sure he wasn't injured; the firefighters began the firefighter banter as we always do to our own. Shakey, visibly upset, told them he had only purchased liability on the truck and had no insurance to replace the truck.

The police when they got there called the power company to come clean up the mess the accident had caused. Shakey was worried about the light poles and if his insurance would pay to replace them. Thankfully, his son, Larry, worked for the power company, and Shakey called him to come pick him up and take him home. When Larry got there, the power company was already on the scene. They told Larry that they were scheduled to replace all these poles and his dad taking them out helped them, so they wouldn't charge him for them. Shakey was relieved and soon went and bought another truck.

The truck, a 1989 Chevy half-ton with a nice graphic pattern on it, is now part of Irving Fire Department lore. The evening of the day Shakey picked up the truck from the dealership, he picked up Ginger for their first date.

Ginger told me, "He gave me our first kiss inside that truck."

"It didn't take him long to kiss you," as I looked at Shakey.

"Well, why wait, I knew I was going to marry her," Shakey replied.

When I went over to Shakey's house for my first interview for the book, I saw the truck in the driveway. "Surely this is not the same truck when you drove when you worked for the fire department?" I asked Shakey.

"Yeah, it is. It has over 400,000 miles on it. (474,353 to be exact) The guy who changes my oil says that he has never seen a gasoline engine with that many miles on it."

"Do you still drive it?"

"Sure, I haven't started it for a couple of weeks, but it will start." As he pulled his keys out of his pocket and climbed in and sure enough it started, as he started revving the engine.

Laughing I said, "No one on the fire department will believe this." And they didn't.

Shakey's everyday driver with 474,353 miles.

I posted the story on Facebook and got over 1,000 likes. Shakey is an amazing generous man, and his legend grows, as he is still driving "the truck."

RUNNING WITH THE BULLS

Run of a Lifetime. Shakey and Charlie before the run.

S hakey was always very competitive, tough and up for a challenge no matter the situation. One morning before my shift, I went to the training academy to play a game of pick-up basketball. If Benji Cox was there with Bob Klassen, multiple people would usually get hurt by flying elbows. I called it casketball instead of basketball. Shakey showed up that morning to play and we were on opposing teams. Shakey got in my face, looked me right in the eye, and said, "I'm guarding you."

A little background to the story: We were on opposite sides of the fence about an issue with the Fire Association. He had just won the presidency, and I was the treasurer. We didn't see eye-to-eye on how things should be *concerning the association. So, the game got a little competitive between the two of us.*

Shakey is 20 years my senior, and I was in pretty good shape and confident of my abilities as a basketball player. We played a couple games of full court casketball, and Shakey never once was not right in the middle of my chest, guarding me the whole time. As I drove to the station, tired, sore, and needing a quick hot shower, I grew in my admiration of this legend. I wondered how he had the stamina to guard me like he did.

His legend grew again when Shakey turned 70 and boarded a plane to fly to Pamplona, Spain, with Ginger and their friends, Jean and Charlie Hicks, to go run with the bulls.

A Spanish Tradition

The running of the bulls is a nine-day event held every year, and the festival is in honor of the martyred Saint Fermin. This Spanish tradition dates to the 14th Century and has become a global event. The tradition began when the bulls were moved from the fields outside of town to the city to sell them, or for bullfights. Young men were hired to chase the bulls into the city. Soon it became a competition with the dumb men running in front of the bulls to try and beat them to the bullpens. Cities all over Spain have these competitions, but the most popular running of the bulls is held every July 6-14 in Pamplona, Spain.

There are rules to follow to run with the bulls. You must be over the age of 18 and run in the same direction as the bulls. You cannot incite the bulls, and you cannot be under the influence of alcohol. The city erects wooden fences along the narrow streets of the 957-yard route. The event begins each day with the runners singing a benediction and ending in "Viva San Fermin!" (Long live Saint Fermin!)

All runners dress in the traditional clothing of the festival run, which consists of white shirt and trousers and a red waistband and neckerchief. You also carry the day's newspaper rolled up to distract the bulls when they get too close by hitting them with it. Only if you touch a bull can you claim you actually ran with the bulls.

The race starts with an 8 a.m. rocket blast. When you hear the second rocket, the six bulls and six steers (they use the same steers each day to lead the bulls to the bullring) have been released and the third rocket tells everyone all the bulls have entered the bullring and you have survived the run. The average speed of the herd of bulls is 15 mph, and every year from 50 to 100 people are transported to the hospital.[4]

A Lifelong Dream

The Holders and Hicks were great friends and traveled together all the time. Shakey had introduced Ginger's best friend, Jean, to Charlie, and they were married. Shakey recounted this about Charlie. "He had an interesting life. He was friends with John F. Kennedy before he became president of the United States, and they remained friends after he was elected."

One night at dinner with their wives, Charlie asked, "Shakey, let's go run with the bulls in Spain."

Shakey said, "Why would I go do that?"

"It's a lifelong dream of mine. I want to do it before I die."

Shakey, thought to himself, *I don't want to die doing something this stupid.*

Charlie stated, "When I was 18, I was there, but got too drunk to run with the bulls. Come on, Shakey, come run with me. Hell, you're a firefighter, running into burning buildings. Anyone stupid enough to run into burning buildings is stupid enough to run with the bulls."

Finally, Shakey relents, "OK, Charlie, I'll go with you and run with those bulls."

Spain

Landing in Spain, they drove to Pamplona to check into a $1,000 per night hotel. After checking in, they walked the streets and took in the sights. The girls went shopping for the uniforms the guys needed to run with the bulls. They headed back to the hotel to get some rest and decided on a time to meet for dinner.

At dinner Shakey begins feeling the tension of running with the bulls, but it was soon forgotten by the time they finished dinner. They went to the bar and joined the party as it was getting louder and louder. There were a bunch of Australians there getting drunk and getting ready for the run tomorrow morning.

Shakey asked one of them, "Do you do anything special to get ready for the run?"

"No, just drink for three days is all we do."

Recounting that night, Shakey says, "The bar was packed, and everyone was partying and having a good time, just getting really drunk. They began playing a Spanish song, and everyone was singing the song in Mexican. I couldn't understand them, but the song had the same tune as the Australian song, *Singing with Matilda*. Everyone was spilling their beers and having a really big time." (This song's actual name was *Waltzing Matilda*.)

Shakey looked at Ginger and decided it was best to leave the party and get some rest for the next day. They said goodnight to Charlie and Jean. Shakey jumped up and grabbed Ginger with glee as he comes waltzing Ginger, down the hallway, with me, as all the drunk Australians are singing the chorus:

> *Down came a jumbuck to drink at the billabong*
> *Up jumped the swagman and grabbed him with glee*
> *He sang as he shoved that jumbuck in his tucker bag*
> *"You'll come a-Waltzing Matilda, with me!"*
> *Waltzing Matilda, waltzing Matilda*
> *"You'll come a-Waltzing Matilda, with me!"*
> *He sang as he shoved that jumbuck in his tucker bag*
> *"You'll come a-Waltzing Ginger, with me!"*

Breakfast Warning

The next morning, the four of them woke up early and met for breakfast. Charlie and Shakey had on their white pants and shirts, with a red sash around their waists and necks that the girls had bought the day before. No one had slept well, anticipating the run. They ordered coffee and looked at the menu. Shakey was his usual self, talking fast and planning his attack. He had done this all his adult life, running into the depths of life and death situations as a firefighter. The firefighter's motto was always, "everyone goes home safe," and that was his plan this day. The women who served breakfast came up to the table.

"Are you going to run today?"

"Yeah, we are going to run," replied Shakey.

"Well, I advise you not to run."

"Why?"

"Because 90 percent of the people who get hurt each year are Americans."

"Why is that?"

"Because they are drunk and stupid!"

Shakey looked at Charlie and then at the wives. All are thinking, *hopefully, this is not our last meal together.*

Run of a Lifetime

Shakey and Charlie and the wives made their way down to the street where the start of the race begins. There was a mass of stupid humanity walking with them. Shakey's mind flashed to all the close calls he had as a firefighter. He was thinking how stupid this could be. There was some small talk, and the two combatants kissed their brides, still hoping it won't be the last time. Shakey and Charlie jumped the fence. Standing in the street, rocking back and forth, a man next to them slurs,

"How old are you?"

Shakey says, "I'm 70."

"What did you do for a living?"

"I'm a firefighter."

"Still a firefighter?"

"Yeah, still a firefighter."

"Man, that's good, mate, maybe you won't die."

Shakey thinks to himself, *you are too drunk to run, and where is your shirt?*

"That bull is going to gore you and you are going to wish you had your shirt on," Shakey said.

"No mate, all a shirt will do is get tangled with the bull's horn and not let me get away from him. This is my third time to run and my mates back in Australia can't see me on TV. I want the people back home to see me on TV, running with these bulls. Safe run, mate!"

The rocket went off and the mob of people began running. They shoved each other, and people fell to the ground and were getting trampled, both by bulls and people. When those bulls were about 50 yards from catching up with them, Shakey told Charlie, "I am stupid."

Shakey's firefighter training kicks in and he pulls Charlie into the doorway, out of harm's way. The bulls charge through the crowd and pass on. People were yelling and waving their newspapers frantically. The bulls rounded a wet pavement corner and began slipping and sliding and falling, with more people getting hurt. Charlie took off running with Shakey, following in the mass of humanity. Shakey passed people lying in the street, bleeding and already being attended to by the medical teams. He looked down and saw a man bleeding out his ear as he continues running down the street.

"Geez, where is a bull I can swat?" Shakey yelled.

Shakey had lost Charlie in the crowd, but he didn't care. He had one thing on his mind—his main goal—to swat a bull with his newspaper. He saw there were a couple of bulls still trying to gain their hooves on the wet pavement. The bulls were horning anyone in front of them as they continued their rampage to the arena. Then Shakey saw his chance. With his heart thumping in his chest, he ran and swatted a bull as the bull got up off the pavement.

The bull thankfully turned and began running toward the stadium, trampling everyone in his path. Shakey's adrenaline was pumping and so were his feet as he continued his quest to run all the way to the stadium. The bulls were tired and slowed by the crowded gate into the arena, so Shakey could follow alongside them with the mass of other runners. He continued running all the way into the bullring, exuberant with pride.

He immediately began looking for Charlie and the girls and spotted them on the other side of the fence. He ran over to them and climbed the fence, super excited he had survived and didn't die. He told them all that had happened, talking so fast because he was still filled with adrenaline, that he spit his false teeth out. Charlie, Jean, and Ginger laughed as Shakey bent down, scrambling to grab his teeth and put them back in his mouth and finish his story of swatting a bull.

It was a great morning for me, sitting with Ginger and Shakey, drinking coffee and eating Ginger's carrot cupcakes, having this legend retell his story of running with the bulls.

MILLIONAIRE TWICE OVER
AND OVER AND OVER

When Shakey finally retired, he received a large severance of over $900,000 from the City of Irving, which included compensation from his unused sick leave and his drop money from his pension. Matt Smith, Shakey's long time driver at Station 1, tried to convince Shakey to roll this money into some kind of investment so he could shelter the money and not have to pay as much tax to the government.

"I've made plenty of money in my life; at this age I just can't afford to lose any more of it," Shakey told Matt.

Shakey paid the 40% taxes he owed and put the rest of his retirement money in the bank where the average yield was .054 APY.

His sister, Margie, in our conversation with her, said, "My brother could have been a millionaire twice over if he had collected all the unpaid rent his tenants owed him over the years."

Another Couple Millions

I've already told you that Shakey had always been successful in everything he had ever done, except for one thing and that was his first marriage to Ruby. Shakey estimated the cost of the divorce to be $680,000, which was in 1983. He determined the value of the six rent houses, the 140-acre Holder farm behind the Denison dam for Lake Texoma, the house on the farm and the house in Grand Prairie by looking at the tax roll. In today's market it would be worth well over two million dollars. Shakey ended the story by saying,

"My whole marriage with Ruby I had a headache, and carried a bottle of aspirin in my truck and took them all the time. Since then, with Ginger, I've not taken any aspirin."

Ponzi Scheme

"Compared to today's notorious cons, the loss associated with this scam in 1920 might seem a pittance. But in the tale of Charles Ponzi, it wasn't just the size of the swindle but the speed with which it was done. According to Smithsonian Magazine, *Ponzi made an estimated $15 million in eight months by convincing lenders he could make them rich with investments in international postal reply coupons. His story was so infamous that the basics of the pyramid scheme—take money from a new investor to pay back an old one—began to carry his name, despite the fact that he wasn't the first to do it."*[5]

Another Million Gone

Bernard (Bernie) Ebbers founded WorldCom, the USA's second-largest internet phone company, in 1999. Ginger's father was one of the original investors in the company. He knew Ebbers through his daughter, Carolyn, who socialized in those circles in Mississippi. Ginger's dad didn't put a lot of money in the WorldCom stocks, but his investment grew to $10 million. He continued to tell his son-in-law to invest, and Shakey finally began investing $10,000 several times over a period of a year. His investment grew rapidly. Unfortunately, it turned out to be a Ponzi scheme orchestrated by its founder Bernie Ebbers.

Shakey and firefighter Jim Caudle, who was his tailboard, were hanging out a lot after Shakey's divorce and after he married Ginger. Jim started getting suspicious trying to warn Shakey this could be a scam. Then the scandal broke in June of 2002. Ebbers had orchestrated a scheme to inflate earnings to maintain WorldCom stock prices.

Jim began warning Shakey to get out and at least complete his goal of paying off the new house. Shakey had bought Ginger her Mississippi dream home for $250,000 in McKinney.

Bernie Ebbers personally invited Shakey and Ginger to fly down to Florida and stay in his beach house. He told them they couldn't close him down because he had too many assets. Ebbers invited them out on his private yacht, which he had just bought and with a large crew, and wined and dined them in the Gulf. Shakey's investment was now almost a million dollars and Jim kept pleading with him to at least fulfill his goal of paying off the new house.

When I talked to Jim, he recalled, "The stubborn goat wouldn't sell and lost everything." Shakey's father-in-law lost $10 million in the scandal. World Com admitted that it had overstated its assets by over $11 billion and at the time it the largest accounting fraud in U.S. history.

"The stock went to two cents a share. I still have the stocks in my office," Shakey said.

"I was sick to my stomach over them losing all that money," added Ginger.

"Aw, just make some more, heck, I can make more," said Shakey.

Just another incredible legendary story about Shakey, you must ponder.

THE "C" WORD

No one wants to hear they have cancer. Most, if not all of us, have had loved ones or friends who have departed this life with cancer. My wife is a breast cancer survivor, and I lost my step-dad and mother to the awful disease. As a department, Irving has a high rate of cancer among our retirees. I spoke to Mike Harris, a retired fire prevention specialist and fire investigator, who worked 30 years for the Irving Fire Department. He headed up our public education sector and started our Citizen Fire Academy.

After retirement Mike contracted cancer; thankfully, it is in remission. After contracting the dreaded disease, he began compiling a list of Irving firefighters who currently have cancer. We have 41 who are fighting sixteen different cancers. Eleven have prostate cancer, six with multiple myeloma, four with leukemia, one with bone cancer, five with melanoma, one with basal cell carcinoma, one with colon cancer, three with lymphoma, one with testicular cancer, one with solitary plasma cytoma, one with lung cancer, one with high grade sarcoma, two with rectal cancer, one with skin cancer, one with stomach cancer, and one with throat cancer. The number of my brother firefighters who lost their battle against this "nemesis" is also a large and painful list.

SCBAs

The culture in the early years of the fire service was to fight fires aggressively, with a quick interior attack and with little or no thought of their own safety. The department at that time had only one SCBA (self-contained breathing apparatus) on an engine at Central Fire Station. Its purpose was to put it on any victim they found in a fire before dragging them to safety. It never happened.

According to Firefighter Ronnie Mayo," When they did issue SCBAs for everyone, no one wore them. One reason we didn't, chief hated to go to Dallas FD to have the bottles refilled, so we didn't wear them."

When I joined the department, we were mandated to wear them in all fires, but few officers would put their masks on in an interior fire attack. Now, with education and enforced rules and regulations, all wear their SCBA's, even in overhaul. (Overhaul occurs after the fire is out, and we are looking for hotspots that could rekindle a fire. It is time consuming, but an absolute necessity.)

Purple Haze

Once Shakey and I were on a large fire at a trucking company, where two semi-truck trailers filled with small containers of liquid and granular fertilizer caught fire. The smoke from the fire was a greenish purple in color and heavy inside the trailer. Most had their SCBAs on while fighting the fire, but since it was mainly an outside attack, no one donned their mask. After the fire was brought under control, the Battalion Chief ordered the two trailers to be overhauled. There were a lot of newly hired rookies for Station 7 (that hadn't opened yet), so we got the "pleasure" to overhaul. We all donned our SCBA's and masked up and began shoveling debris out of the trailer and onto the warehouse dock. The Battalion Chief, wanting to clear more crews, ordered us to remove our SCBAs so we could "work faster." While shoveling, and with a lot of trepidation, the Jimi Hendrix song rang in my mind, "Purple Haze."

Many Dangers

Our career as firefighters is dangerous in so many ways. Some of the many dangers we could encounter might be a car fire on the highway in rush-hour traffic. We never wore our SCBAs on these fires. How about a large trash container at a commercial business that is on fire, with no telling what's in it? Then you have a myriad of hazardous material spill calls. They call them hazardous for a reason, and many could possibly cause cancer. Or medical runs, which are the majority of our incidents, that have all sorts of contagious possibilities. When I joined the department in 1981, it was the beginning of the AIDS epidemic. It was tragic in so many ways. We were scared not only for our patients, but for our safety. We handled it with professionalism, courage, and compassion. Shakey and the department fought many fires in large businesses filled with all kinds of harmful materials. These and other dangers, firefighters must handle at a moment's notice, and each incident has some effect on your overall health, both physically and mentally.

A New Motto

Thankfully, the department and the City of Irving have made monumental strides to protect firefighters' safety with funding and education. One huge change in the fire service for the better is the cleaning of our gear after a fire. It was a badge of honor if your helmet and fire coat were covered with the black soot of smoke. Many helmets were visibly distorted by the heat of a fire. After a fire, we would come into the station with our bunker pants on, covered with debris of the fire, and drink a glass of sweet tea, telling war stories about the fire. This brought all that contamination inside the station. We would eventually go outside, hose off the large chunks of sheetrock and insulation on our gear and hang it on the engine for the next "one." We would handle the gear for days with our hands absorbing carcinogens into our bodies and/or mouths.

Now, every firefighter has two sets of fire gear. There are no more garden hose cleanings. They are professionally cleaned. Also, we had the smell of diesel exhaust from the fire equipment that filled the firehouse on a daily basis. The city finally began installing large exhaust fans in the apparatus room to evacuate the hazard. This really was only a Band-Aid measure.

Now, all equipment, when backing into the station, has PlyoVents connected to the fire engine's exhaust that captures the diesel exhaust before it enters the station. The firefighters' motto was "Everyone goes home." We needed to add the word "healthy." This new generation of firefighters will have a much greater chance of hopefully living a long life without the "C" word.

Something is Not Right!

After one hard day of working on a vacant rent house, Shakey walked into the house and found Ginger in their bedroom.

"Geez, I'm tired. I can barely take my clothes off. Driving home I wasn't tired, but started feeling really tired before I got here," Shakey said.

"That's not like you. Maybe you should stay home tomorrow and not go to the station," replied Ginger.

"Aw, it ain't nothing. Besides, we have to go take our physicals tomorrow."

Shakey showered as Ginger prepared him something to eat. Later that evening they went to bed. The next morning, like every third day, Shakey got up and put on his station uniform, trying not to wake Ginger. He headed to his truck and couldn't wait to get to the station and be with his crew, serving the citizens of Irving.

He relieved Captain Kirby, put his gear on the engine, and walked into the station. "We have to be at the doctor's office by 10 o'clock for our physical, so after breakfast, let's get the house cleaned before we go," he said to his crew.

Later they headed to the engine and stowed their gear. Shakey climbed in and grabbed the radio mic, "Injun One, clear, enroute to hospital for our physicals."

Dispatch responded, "Engine 1, clear."

They all finished their exams, and while driving back to the station, Shakey was thinking, *I'm still more tired than normal. My vitals were all good. No temperature. But something is not right.*

Bad News

The biannual physical report two years earlier showed his white blood cells were a little elevated. The doctor asked Shakey if he had a cold or a sore throat. He had responded that he was just getting over a cold. The doctor said, "That's probably why your white blood cells are a little elevated and not to worry."

Two weeks after his recent physical, the doctor called Shakey at the station and asked if he could come to his office when he got off work the next morning.

Shakey replied, "Sure, I can come by on the way home."

That night Shakey and his crew made a couple of medical calls and when they got back, Shakey climbed back in bed, but had trouble falling back to sleep.

The next morning the station speakers opened to announce, "0700 hours." Shakey got up and dressed, went, and got a cup of coffee. After pouring a cup, he went to the captain's office to make sure his crew had filled out their reports and C Shift captain relieved him. Shakey grabbed his shaving kit and took a quick shower before leaving to go to the doctor's office.

Leaving the Station and driving to the hospital, Shakey wondered what this could be about. He parked his truck, walked into the lobby, pushed the up arrow, and as the elevator door opened, he walked in. Arriving on the second floor, he walked into the doctor's office and told the receptionist that the doctor wanted to see him. She asked him to have a seat and said, 'We'll call you back shortly.'

Shakey was now sitting in the examining room. The doctor walked in and shook Shakey's hand. There was a long pause. The doctor, looking into Shakey's eyes, said, "I don't know how to tell you, Shakey, other than you have cancer."

Shakey replies, "No kidding."

"And it's in the fourth stage."

"Geez, I never ever thought about having cancer ... how can we fix it?"

The doctor says, "I know a good oncologist, Dr. Perkins; I recommend you go see him as soon as you can."

This was May 2005.

Telling Ginger and His Crew

On the way home, Shakey tried to digest the news he had received. He walked into the house, and Ginger was there and could tell immediately that something was wrong. As she looked at Shakey, he told her the bad news, that he had cancer. Ginger, extremely worried, tried to get Shakey to tell her all the doctor had said to him.

"He wants me to go see a doctor named Perkins."

"Shakey, how bad is it?"

"The doctor said it was stage four. Let's call Dr. Perkins' office and see when I can get in to see him."

Ginger agreed and said, "We also need to call the kids and tell them."

"Call the doctor first and then we'll drive over to Cindy's house and tell her, and we can call Larry and Rick this evening."

How to Tell His Crew

The next shift came and Shakey got up early and drove to the station. He relieved the captain and started his shift like he always did, writing in the logbook those who were on duty. Sitting in his office chair, he rears back with his hands behind his head, thinking of all the possibilities of the biggest opponent he has ever had to face. *How much he liked coming to the station and being a firefighter ... fighting fires and saving lives ... riding the engine with lights and sirens blaring ... the many people he has met and helped ... and how he should tell his crew.* It was Matt's (his Driver and one of his closest friends) day off, so he knew he needed to call him also. His mind was spinning.

The guys fixed a big breakfast and yelled at Shakey that breakfast was ready. Shakey came out of the office, and they all could tell something was wrong. They ate breakfast with Shakey not saying much, and when he had finished, he stood, went over and slid his plate in the sink. He turns to his crew and says,

"Guys, I've got cancer. The doctor called last shift and told me to come to his office. When I got to there, he told me."

The crew stood there for a moment looking at each other in disbelief.

He quietly said, "Let's get the house cleaned up before we have to go do those school drills at 9:30."

The rest of the shift was solemn as each thought about the fight they would all be in with their captain.

His Men's Reactions

Alan Herd was driving the engine that day. He recalled, "Shakey did a really good job of not worrying us with his health issue. He wanted things done as we always did. He carried his load the whole time, like always. He hid his feelings real well—didn't wear them on his shoulders. We all cared deeply for him. It was a hard fight. He was 71 years old. All of us thought he would retire and enjoy what time he had left. But the fire department was what he enjoyed most. He was taking double doses of chemo but missed hardly any days at work. He would take the treatment on the day he got off and be back the next shift. We were all amazed, and my respect for him grew even more."

Matt recalled, "I tried to get Shakey to file a worker's comp claim. I showed him studies that proved diesel exhaust causes this kind of cancer. Shakey kept telling me the fire department and the City had been too good to him all these years to file a claim on them. I told him, 'I know, but you are entitled to the benefits.' He would tell me, 'I'll just pay for the treatments out of my own pocket.'"

"He could have saved himself a lot of money, having to pay for the coverage the insurance didn't cover. He's stubborn, but that was the way he wanted to do it."

Let's Shake on It

Sitting in the doctor's office, Dr. Perkins told Shakey, Ginger and Cindy, "Shakey, you have CLL, chronic lymphocytic leukemia, a type of cancer of the blood and bone marrow." He explained that the spongy tissue inside the bone is where blood cells are made, and that Shakey probably had cancer when his white blood cells were elevated on the last physical exam. It was a slow-growing cancer and could spread to other organs.

Dr. Perkins had gone to a seminar recently and learned about a new experimental drug, and it was having good results treating this cancer. "We need to start your treatment as soon as possible," the doctor said.

Shakey asked, "Will this cure the cancer?"

Dr. Perkins said, "No, there is no cure, we can only manage it. We must also keep it from spreading to other organs. With it being a slow-growing cancer, we can expect you to live a good five to seven years with this stage of cancer."

Cindy had been quiet, listening and taking notes until she heard this prognosis. She cried out, "Wait a minute, Dr. Perkins. We have got to have a better plan, a pact between me and you. This is my daddy, and I need him around till he is 113!"

Dr. Perkins saw how determined Cindy was and finally said, "Okay, let's have this pact."

Cindy reached out her hand and says, "Let's shake on it, till 113 years old, right?" as the two shook hands.

The Fight Was On

Dr. Perkins laid out a very aggressive plan of attack, and the fight was on! He told Shakey, "Normally, I treat my patients with only one treatment a week. That is about all one can handle. But being a firefighter and in such good shape, I think you can handle two treatments a week. Most people get sick and are tired with one treatment. Do you want to try this?"

Shakey, with Cindy shaking her head yes, said, "Yeah, I've been a fighter all my life. Let's do it."

Grueling Battle

Shakey said, "This was the first time I felt depressed in my life." He stayed depressed for about two weeks and then realized to beat this opponent, he had to be positive, fight the cancer, and win this fight. Shakey continued to go to the fire station, work his 24-hour shift, and the next morning he would drive to the hospital for his treatment. The next day he rested at home and went back to the station the following day for his 24-hour shift. He repeated this grueling pattern week after week for a year and a half. Shakey remarkably said he never felt sick while taking the treatments. He only had to take a sick day when a treatment happened to fall on the shift he worked.

We Ain't Doing This Again!

Dr. Perkins ordered a bone marrow test a month into his treatments. They needed to see if the treatments were doing what they were supposed to do. Shakey went in and the doctor explained the procedure.

He asked Shakey, "Do you think you are tough enough to have this with no sedative? He added with emphasis, "You are a firefighter."

After a short time to think about it, Shakey told him he was tough enough. Dr. Perkins began, but about halfway through the procedure, Shakey, gritting his teeth, groaned, "Doc, you better get all you need this time, because I ain't doing this again."

Another Fight

Many of the people who were taking the treatment while Shakey was taking his treatments did not win the fight against this formidable opponent. Shakey continued to see Dr. Perkins, who warned them that the new experimental drug could cause other complications. Shakey also saw a specialist to regularly check for squamous cell carcinoma, which was a side effect of the new experimental drug treatment. He had a lesion appear on the side of his face and went to the specialist, who prescribed a treatment and told him to come back in two weeks.

This was a big mistake because the carcinoma spread rapidly. Shakey's jaw began to hurt, and he called Dr. Perkins's office. Dr. Perkins called Shakey back, and after hearing what was wrong, he had Shakey come to see him immediately. Shakey went to see him and after examining him, Dr. Perkins knew this was serious. He called his good friend who is a foremost expert on these types of cancer at UT Southwestern in Dallas.

Dr. Perkins said to the doctor, "He is 70 years old and in good shape, plus he has good insurance. When can you see him?" It was five o'clock in the afternoon, and the doctor said to send him over right now.

Dr. Perkins' office was in Irving and the new doctor's office was in Dallas. Traffic was always bad at that time of day, but the doctor waited. When they finally got there, the doctor saw the problem and said, "We must operate as soon as we can."

A team of doctors was assembled for a 13-hour operation. New blood vessels to the area were needed. A skin graft from the inner thigh was placed over the open wound next to his ear, followed by other complicated procedures. It was an exhausting day for everyone involved. As a result of the procedure, Shakey lost part of his ear and has some paralysis in that area of the face. Shakey, over the years, has had two other carcinomas removed from his head.

But 18 years and counting, he is cancer-free and a victorious fighter against the "C" word.

While my manuscript was at the proofreader, Shakey spent three days in the hospital with kidney stones that were removed. He was weak after he returned home. He wasn't bouncing back like we all hoped he would, and the family decided to go see Dr. Perkins. After examining Shakey, we got the news that the cancer had come out of remission. Shakey is now in a new fight.

LEE POLLEI

Ira Munday and Travis Eden, heros at the propane fire.

In the fire service, you make lifelong friends, and one of Shakey's best friends is the oldest living firefighter of the Irving Fire Department, Lee Pollei. He turned 92 a few days after my first meeting with him in March 2023. Like Shakey, he was from humble means, growing up in Barkley, Texas. Times were hard and good paying jobs were hard to find.

Lee remarked, "A common laborer was paid a dollar an hour, so if you worked eight hours, you were paid $8, or $10 for ten hours of work. My brother and I worked in a blacksmith shop washing car parts in diesel. We would get paid 25 cents and after work, go to the store and buy a moon pie and RC Cola.

When Lee was a little kid, he would stay with his sister and brother-in-law in Dallas. There was a fire station close by, and Lee would go there sometimes to see the fire trucks and talk to the firefighters. And like a lot of kids, he dreamed of becoming a firefighter one day.

Lee's dream would come true one day, but his first fire he was not able to save the house. His grandma had passed, and his dad went to Temple, Texas, to be with his grandpa.

"Mom had to take care of us boys. (Lee had a younger brother by 15 months.) We didn't grow up with a lot of discipline. One day we were smoking hand-rolled cigarettes in the outdoor toilet. We threw the cigarettes on the wood floor to stomp it out, but one must have fallen through one of the cracks. Afterward, we went to town and while we were there, someone yelled, 'There's a fire down at the Pollei's.'"

The two brothers ran as fast as they could and tried to put the fire out with buckets of water from a garden hose. The fire spread to the high grass around the outhouse, and the outhouse was a total loss. The boys knew they were in trouble when their dad got home, so they had to go buy a new one. The only outhouse they could buy had a door that swung opposite of the one they had burned up, and they knew their dad would know. They brought it home anyway (their momma had to have a place to do her business) and got it operational where the old one was. They cut all the tall grass around it and began watering the common Bermuda so it would be green.

Lee was learning about fire prevention at an early age!

Waiting for a Civil Service Job

Like a lot of men in those days, Lee joined the Army to serve his country. He said, "It was the best thing that ever happened to me. You learned discipline and respect for your elders, how to follow leadership, and how to fight. You have to learn to love and respect each other just to stay alive. We were a team." After returning home from the war, he married Jackie.

Lee told his family he was going to Dallas to look for work. When Lee got to Dallas, he met a guy who asked him what he was planning to do. I told him, "I've come here looking for a civil service job, so I'll always have a job. I want to be either a firefighter, work for the post office, or for the police department."

As fate would have it, the man replies, "My uncle works in Irving at the City Shop, and they are hiring firefighters for a new fire station." It was Fire Station 3 on Grauwyler Road.

Lee hurried home to tell Jackie about meeting this man and that he was going to Irving to talk to him about the job. The next morning Lee drove to Irving and met Joe Holloway at the City Shop. After the two talked about the possibility of Lee coming to work for the city, Joe called Chief Cronan and told him there was a veteran out here at the shop wanting to be a firefighter. The chief told him he needed to pick something up at the shop and would come over to meet him. Cronan drove out to the shop and Joe introduced Lee to the chief.

After some small talk, Cronan says, "Let's go downtown to my office and sit down and talk about you becoming one of my firefighters." Lee went to his car and followed Chief Cronan downtown. Chief and Lee pulled their cars into the parking lot in the rear of the Central Fire Station. They walked through the apparatus room and up the stairs to Cronan's office. They talked awhile and then Cronan found an application and handed it to him. He went home and told Jackie, "I need to pass this test to become a firefighter."

Lee still needed to provide for Jackie and their baby, so the next day he drove over to the post office in Irving to see if they were hiring. This was December of 1956, and they informed him they were hiring for the Christmas rush. Lee started the next day delivering mail. Lee came home and told Jackie, "Coming to Irving was the best thing that could have happened to us."

Now a Firefighter

Lee had passed the entrance exam and was hired when Station 3 opened. Chief Cronan called Lee and told him to come to his office and sign some papers and get his gear. After Lee signed his papers, the chief told him, "You will be working here at Central with Captain Red Whaley and his crew." The next day Lee drove downtown and walked into the Station to begin his career. Shakey Holder greeted him with a firm handshake, and this was the beginning of their long friendship.

The early days of the fire department, the men worked a 24-hour-on and 24-hour-off schedule, with only a four-man crew and the 20 volunteers. Since Irving was one of the fastest growing cities in Texas, they quickly added two more stations to serve their citizens. The department trained constantly to be able to handle the occasional fire, car wrecks and lots of grass fires that included the county's property, and all other emergencies. Lee stated, "The trains passing through town were always setting large grass fires.

"Also, the 20 volunteers were not happy with the paid firefighters at first. This was because they weren't going to be the first ones at a fire."

Lee said, "But over time they saw how dedicated we were to our job and to the citizens. We learned to work great together at fires."

Driving to a Fire for the First Time

At Central Station they had a 1951 Chevrolet Tanker that carried 300 gallons of water, a 1936 International grass wagon with 750-gallon water tank, a 1954 Ford with a 150-gallon water tank, and a 1951 Mack truck with a 150-gallon water tank. The city also didn't have a lot of fire hydrants, so the much-needed water to put out a fire was at a premium. Captain Whaley and Shakey taught Lee that you had to get to a fire quickly and attack the fire as fast as you could.

"The best you could hope for in a lot of fires we fought was to get inside and knock the fire down with a reel line and the small amount of tank water. We needed the second engine to get there with more water to fully extinguish the fire," Shakey said.

Shakey also reminisced, "Ira Munday kept putting his fires out with his tank water. The other firefighters called him lucky, but after 20 years of putting out fires, I don't think it was luck; he was just GOOOD."

Lee's second day on the job they had a call for a house fire. He was told that morning if they had a house fire, he was to drive the grass wagon, and Shakey would be driving the engine. The day began with breakfast and morning chores, when dispatch opened the station speakers, dispatching them to a structure fire. Lee dropped his mop on the kitchen floor and followed Shakey, sliding down the fire pole to the apparatus room. Dispatch gave them the address, and with his heart racing and adrenaline pumping, Lee raced to the bay door. He bent over and flung the apparatus bay door up. As he turned to get in the Driver's seat, suddenly, the bay door came crashing back down to the floor.

"I was so excited about my first-time driving, I opened it too hard," Lee recalled. He went back and opened it, climbed into the fire truck, pushed the clutch in and started the engine. He pulled the engine out onto the street and looked left to see that Shakey was long gone. Being new to the city, Lee didn't know all the streets.

"I saw them go down Jefferson and headed that way. When I got to Sixth Street, I saw some water on the road. That engine when you turned hard would slosh water out of the tank, so I knew they turned there. Then, when I got to Senter (Street), I saw more water where they had turned. I had the cireen (siren) blaring and the engine started to cut out. As a firefighter you had to learn the trucks and how to drive them. If you blew the cireen (siren) too long on the Grass Wagon, it would quit running because it would take the fire from the spark plugs." Lee finally found the house and, thankfully, it was only a small fire that was already out. But this experience made Lee determined to learn all the streets in the city.

Traditions Passed on to the Next Generation

Back at the Station, Lee had gone to Shakey and told him of his plan to learn all the streets and where the hydrants were. Shakey told him, "I've been here two years and don't know all of them; let's start driving them when we get off in the morning."

They began making their own map books that had every street and with the block splits and where the hydrants were located. They also drew floor plans of the buildings and added them to their map book.

Shakey, Lee Pollei and Ira Munday and many others set the course of the Irving Fire Department. A department that cares deeply for the citizens and businesses of Irving and just as importantly, takes care of each other in times of need.

DON BURROWS

D on Burrows began his career with the Irving Fire Department in May of 1967, with a starting salary pay of $410 per month. On his first day at work, he walked into Station 3 and met his first officer, Lieutenant Rex Faulkner. He worked in every fire station Irving had, but most of his career was spent at Station 1. He retired in July of 1994, with Shakey Holder as his captain, serving the citizens of Irving for 27 years. When he was hired, the city had four fire stations, and they were building Station 5 at the corner of Shady Grove Road and Glenwick Lane.

Transferred to One

After a few years, he was eligible to take the driver's test and finished second on the eligibility list, behind Danny Nunn. Don recalled, "I had been driving 'out of class,' (term used for a firefighter of a lower rank moving up to the next rank's pay) at Station 1. The assigned driver was off work because of an injury. So, when they promoted me, the chief left me there driving for Joel Price."

Rumors

I asked Don when he first met Shakey. With a little laugh he said, "At Station 2. He was the captain there and Engine 1 had to go there one morning for training. That was my first time to meet him. I had heard lots of stories about Shakey—that he was really strict and hard to work for. But he was not hard to work for, not for me. "At Station 1 we had Don Sears driving the engine, when Chief Spillman transferred Shakey there. The rumors going around the department were Spillman was transferring him there because there were less people there for him to influence. It would be harder for him to have an influence on other people. Sears was really concerned about him coming there, but I told him, 'Let's wait until he gets here, and we can form our own opinion in a week or two.'

"The morning came when Shakey came down here, he walked in and announced, 'They can put me any place they want to. In a week, I'll have this station running just like I had the other.'

"I said in my head, *OK?* and that began a long friendship with Captain Shakey Holder."

"I thought he ran the station the way a station was supposed to be run. One of the first things he did was he gave us a district test, and Sears was a little 'light' on knowing his district. Shakey had made out the test and handed it to us. He put me in the kitchen and Don went to the captain's office. As we were taking the test, Shakey had a visitor come into the station. They went out to the apparatus room and when Shakey came back into the station, we had finished the test. With a little chuckle, Burrows says, "Don had passed the test."

Driving the Girls Around

I asked Don if he had any funny stories that happened at the station. He said, "Not really, to have funny stories you have to have goofballs working for you. We always had good guys working with us. It probably was because Shakey 'ran a tight ship,' with the men knowing what was expected, and they all respected him as their officer."

Don then said, "I have one story. It was before Ginger and Shakey were married. Ginger and her girlfriend, Jean, would come by the Station to visit him. One day Ginger asked if they could go for a ride on the engine. I didn't care one way or the other, Shakey was the boss. I do whatever the captain says."

So Shakey said, "Let's go for a ride, Don."

"Shakey put the girls up front with me and he got in the back with Jim Caudle. We went and rode around the district, and the girls loved it. Then word got out what Shakey had done, and we knew Chief Spillman would probably investigate. The whole department was wanting to see what was going to happen. Spillman was wanting to see if he could get Shakey fired, and they interviewed everyone but me, and I was the one driving the girls around. I knew it was wrong, but if they had interviewed me, I would've had amnesia. Those kinds of things are meant to stay at the station."

With a big chuckle, Don added, "Obviously, Shakey didn't get fired ... he worked longer than the man who was investigating, and Chief Spillman."

Great Advice About Ginger

Don had another story about Shakey and Ginger. "They had been dating for a while and Shakey called me into the office and told me Ginger had a date with another man. Shakey asked me what I thought about her dating this other guy. I told him, 'She is trying to make you jealous, so you will come around and make this relationship work.' I told him what he needed to do is when he got off in the morning, go talk to her and smooth things over with her.

"He then told me, 'You don't know how glad I am to hear you say that.'

"I said, 'Well, Shakey that's the way it is. She don't want him, she loves you.'

"Shakey went over to her house the next morning and told her that I said he needed to get down on his knee and apologize, but I never said that."

Can't Replace Experience

Every good fire officer needs and has experience, learning with each fire we fight and other emergencies we have been dispatched to. Then returning to the Station, you have a critique of each fire around the kitchen table with your men. You discuss what could have been done differently, what would have been a textbook attack. As you drive home the next morning, sore and tired, you are still fighting the fire in your mind. EXPERIENCE— it's all about experience in the fire service.

Shakey's experience was on full display by a fire they had on Second Street. Engine 1 was dispatched and with lights and sirens, they raced to see what they had. As they pulled up in front of the house, Shakey was running through his mind, single-story house ... dark smoke ... still coming out ... no visible fire ... we have one ... It's time to put another fire out.

Don recounted, "We were met in the front yard by two men who lived there, and they immediately said, 'The fire is out.' I mentally agreed with them. Shakey didn't. He ordered our firefighter to go pull an inch and half hose line and Shakey went to the front door. He stepped inside and encountered a room of total darkness and intense heat. He turned and yelled, 'Don, this fire isn't out; it's in the attic, get us some water.'"

"I got them water and Shakey pulled a hole in the ceiling, exposing a roaring fire in the attic. Our firefighter started attacking the fire with Shakey guiding him the whole time and they were able to black the fire out."

Shakey's years of experience was on display as the IFD put another fire out.

I Didn't Know I Was Driving

Don told a story about a major accident he and Shakey had on southbound Loop 12. It was a cold winter evening with snow and ice on the roads. They saw the accident as a man in front of them began to slow down in light traffic. Don carefully arrived at the scene of the accident and stopped. As he was reaching for the knob to the air brakes, he glanced in his rearview mirror. There, he saw a car coming too fast, and turned to Shakey and yelled, "This car is going to hit us."

Sure enough, they feel the impact of the crash. The police were already on the scene and Shakey gets out of the engine and hollers to the officer, "This idiot hit us."

"I saw him," the officer replied to Shakey, as Shakey and Don walked back to see if the man was hurt and how much damage was done to the engine.

"The police officer began his investigation by asking the driver, 'Were you following more than 500 feet behind that fire engine?'

"He slurred, 'I didn't know I was driving.'

"The officer reaching for his handcuffs said to him, 'Turn around and put your hands behind your back.'

As Don and Shakey walked back to the front of engine, Don moaned, "Guess we will be going to the Accident Review Board." Shakey shook his head in agreement and disgust.

Accident Review Board

No one wants to have an accident. It is really a big hassle for everyone at the Station. You have to swap all your equipment over to a much older reserve engine however long it takes to repair the damage on the front-line engine. And almost as bad is having to write a memo that details what happened in a way that won't get you in more trouble. The review board reviews the evidence of the accident, and you may receive a reprimand that goes into your file, or if serious, time off without pay, or vindication if you are lucky.

The day came for Engine 1 to go before the Accident Review Board. Shakey, Don, and their tailboard got their gear stowed on the engine, dreading the process of meeting with the review board.

As Don started the engine, Shakey grabbed the mic and said to Dispatch, "Injun (engine) 1 clear to Accident Review Board with a brand-new rope."

"Receive Engine 1, Engine 1 enroute to City Hall with brand new rope."

Don and Shakey went to the conference room on the third floor and were met at the door by Chief Pritchett. He told Don and Shakey to have a seat and he began the interview. He informed them that he had read their memos, and they would go into their files. He then asked Shakey,

"Was there anything you could have done to prevent this accident?"

Shakey looked him in the eye and said, "Yes sir, I coulda called in sick that morning."

Don, snickering and with a twinkle in his eye, told me, "That answer didn't go over too good with Pritchett, but that's how it was working for Shakey Holder."

I asked Don his final thoughts about Shakey.

He said, "As a person he is hard-headed as a goat, but he is a good guy. He always stood up for what he believed; he wouldn't change that. He was a good guy and easy to work for. I worked for him for 17 years. We would go on vacation together. He was always good to me and a good friend."

MIKE "STICK" WORTHINGTON

I rang the doorbell at Fire Station 2, Irving's busiest station, and was greeted by two young, eager firefighters. I asked, "Is Worthington here?" They let me in, and I saw the men setting the table for dinner. The two rookies, looking at each other, replied, "He is in a meeting in his office." I told them, "I hung out here for 34 years; what are you having for dinner?"

Memories flooded my mind of great firehouse meals and good times around the kitchen table.

Deep Emotion

After some small talk in the kitchen with the men, two worried-looking rookies came out of the captain's office and Stick greeted me with a handshake and said, "What are you doing here, captain? Did you ride your Harley?"

"Yeah, it's parked out front," I replied.

We walked outside and as Stick checked out the bike, I said, "I'm writing a book about Shakey, and he wanted me to interview you."

Stick replied, "Let's go to my office."

As we walked into the Station, I saw the firefighters already eating some thick bone-in pork chops and said to Stick, "Don't you want to eat first?"

"No, I would rather do this."

We went to Stick's office and sat down. After talking about Firefighter Robert Wesson moving and not having room at his new place for his Harley and giving it to Mike to take care of it, I asked, "What are your thoughts of Shakey?"

Mike visibly swelled up with deep emotions, paused for a moment and said, "Shakey was my mentor, my coach. He has given me more fatherly advice than my father ever did. My mother said one time ... I had worked for Shakey around seven years at this time, and I was always talking to her about something he had done for me. My own mom said she thought that Shakey had been more of a dad than my dad ever was. My dad was a good dad, but he wasn't there much. That was my mom's perception, based on what she had heard me say about Shakey. She never met him, and I regret that."

Never Doubt Me Again

"When I first went to One's [Station], the tone was set very quickly. That afternoon, we had a transformer fire, and it was burning. This old man told me, 'Get a hose off there and spray water on it.' I stood there a second and hadn't said anything, but I guess by the look on my face, he knew I had doubts. Shakey ordered me, 'Get that hose line and spray water on it.' As I dragged the line toward the fire, Shakey reassured me, 'I will never tell you to do anything that will get you hurt.' I paused and sheepishly laughed, 'I was going to do it, captain.' He then said, 'I know you are going to do it, but don't ever doubt what I tell you.' What he said to me that day has stuck in my mind, and I never doubted him again."

What Would Shakey Do?

"Shakey wasn't my first captain; I worked for him from 1996-2006. In those early years, we rode three (firefighters) on an engine, so it was me and Shakey alone on a bunch of house and apartment fires. (Station 1 is in old South Irving and on the eastern edge of the city. They also had two large chemical plants in their district. The department closed Central Fire Station, leaving Station 1, a long way from help on any emergency.)

"I had so much respect for the man that I told him I would never promote until he retired. Shakey was old then so I really thought he would retire soon. He was well into his second 20 years (on the department). Then he came down with cancer, and he had a real hard battle with that, so I finally started to study.

"Shakey had these pool parties. They got too big for his backyard, so we started having them over at my house. Shakey was always the first one there. He came in and saw my books where I had been studying and asked me what I was doing. I told him I was studying ... and I said, 'I told you I would never promote,' but he interrupted me before I could finish what I was going to say. He said, 'You better study and promote.' Years later I realized he said that to me because he didn't want to hold me back from furthering my career. When I promoted, it was a bitter pill to swallow.

"I've been a captain for seven years now and when I have a decision to make on the fire ground or at the station, I always think, *what would Shakey do? How would he handle this situation?* Then sometimes I stop and laugh and say to myself, *I don't have the guts to say what Shakey would have said.* I approach the decision I have to make the way he would, but I say it in my way. A good example of how he says things matter-of-factly, but not rudely, was when I brought my new girlfriend to the Station. She was a lot younger than me, and I thought she was a trophy. After she left, Shakey says, 'She's a little chubby, Mike.' At first, I got mad. Then thinking for a second, I say to Shakey, 'She does have some baby fat.' Shakey will say things that are not filtered, but true."

Ding, Ding, Ding

I asked Stick if there was a fire that sticks out in his mind that he and Shakey had fought. With a big laugh he said, "Shakey would kill me if I didn't tell about this fire. We were dispatched to a fire and when we got there, fire was blowing out the front windows. The house was small, about 900 square feet and it was made out of haydite blocks.

"I took the hose to the front door, clicked in my mask and went in. The smoke was black and banked down to my knees and it was really hot. Crawling in I could tell this one could flash. We only had a three-man crew in those days. Typically, I would make entry by myself as Shakey did a quick size-up.

I trusted him and he trusted me, and 100% of the time Shakey would follow the hose in and we would pair up. I started crawling to the right where I knew the fire was, and it was hot as hell. Pulling the line further in, I ran into a chair, and I pushed it out of the way. You couldn't see anything. I pushed further into the darkness, and I ran into something else. After trying to free myself with no luck, I'm starting to panic. Then I thought, *what would Shakey do? He would pull through this.* I kept trying to free myself, but I couldn't, so I began to back out. I then felt Shakey kicking my boot and I muffled a yell through my regulator, 'Is that you Shakey?'

'What's the matter?' Shakey asked.

"I could hear him plainly talking because he didn't have his regulator clicked in. I yelled, 'I'm stuck.'

'What do you mean you're stuck?'

'I'm effin' stuck; I think I'm stuck in a piano stool.'

"Next thing I heard was the ding, ding, ding, ding of the piano keys as Shakey said, 'Yeah, it's a piano.' All I can think of in the middle of this raging inferno fire that is hot as hell, in this small house, is *I'm never going to live this one down for the rest of my career.* And I haven't. I guarantee you at his birthday party next week, his 89th, he will bring this fire up."

Let Me Speak to the Captain

"Another story I have to tell is this one," continued Stick. "One night I'm tired, and I go to bed early. Matt (Smith) and Cass (Williams) are playing this game on the TV in the bedroom. I could cover my head with a pillow and fall asleep with all the noise going on. I can fall asleep anywhere. About an hour later Engine 1 is dispatched to a broken gas line—but I didn't hear the call. They all went and bunked out and Herd yells, 'Stick didn't get up, I'll go get him.' Shakey says, 'If he is that tired, just let him sleep.'

"I'm sleeping and I wake up, hearing the phone ringing and no one is answering it. It keeps ringing and I'm getting mad because I thought they were all in the living room watching TV and playing a joke on me, wanting me to get up and answer it. Finally, I get up and grab the phone and say, 'Station 1, Worthington.' This real important sounding man says, 'Let me speak to the captain.' I say, 'I'll go get him, sir.'

"I go to the living room, and no one is there. I'm starting to panic. I go to the kitchen and look out the window on the kitchen door and don't see the engine. I go out to the apparatus room to see if they had pulled it out on the approach and they are not there. Now I'm really panicking and wondering who this is on the phone. Is it one of the chiefs? So, I have to pick up the phone and I say, 'Sir, can I take a message? The engine is not here right now.'

"Well, the person on the other end starts berating me, 'What do you mean, there is no one there? Are they on a run and you are not on it; why are you not on the run with them?' Then I hear Alan Herd's little girl laugh and say, 'F you, and don't wake me up when y'all get back.'

"I go get back in bed and I'm lying there thinking, *Will Shakey be mad? How much trouble am I in?* Then I hear the warning bell 'beeps' as the engine is backing in. When it gets inside the apparatus room, Matt lays on the horn for about 30 seconds straight. All I could do was lay there and laugh. Shakey walks in, and I get up and say, 'Why didn't you wake me up?' Shakey calmly says, 'If you were that tired, I just let you sleep.'"

Job Well Done

"That's what set Shakey apart—he cares for his men who worked for him. Everyone who worked for him and promoted to captain, he bought them an expensive bronze statue of him. It's awesome and stands about two feet tall. Me, Matt, Herd, and others have got one. When he gave me mine, I couldn't talk. Sorry, I'm choking up now thinking about it. The statue says, *Job well done.* That's why I didn't take a test (to promote) because I was afraid, I might pass the test and have to leave One's and Shakey. When I did finally promote, Jorge Castro got my spot and worked for Shakey until he retired. Every time I see him, he thanks me for promoting and letting him have my spot."

Let's Give Them a Show

Stick finishes his story about Shakey by saying, "He is Superman to me. It is because of his physical fitness and tenacity at his age. It's incredible. We were doing our physical fitness testing for some new recruits, and Shakey had to do it also. I was the one doing the timing for the test. The test is real—and real hard. Three white shirts (what we call chiefs when they shouldn't be there) came to see if Shakey could pass the test. I watch Shakey put all his fire gear on and sling his SCBA over his head and tighten the straps, marveling a man at his age is about to run the test. We have guys a lot younger than him who struggle passing it in the time allotted. Holding the stopwatch as Shakey walks up to me, I whisper, 'Shake, you don't have to worry, I can fudge the time if need be.' He said confidently, "Don't need to, I'm going to give them chiefs a show and show all these young guys how to do it.

"He picks up the 1-1/2" hose, grabs the nozzle and puts it above his head, and leans forward and takes off dragging it to the finish line. He then proceeds to blow through the next parts of the test and comes to the 3" hose pull. He's straining as he positions himself to snap the hose across the line and falls.

"Now I'm worried that he is going to use up all of his time as I watch him struggle to get to his feet. He finally gets up but doesn't have the momentum to snap the hose across the line. He finally does and then completes other parts and heads for the manikin drag. He picks up the dummy and dragging it backward to the finish, he crosses the line and I stop the watch. I look in admiration at his time, 6 minutes and 17 seconds! He was 77 years old. I just ran the test this year and I'm 57 and still in good shape and we had about the same time. Twenty years older than me? That's Superman!

JIN LEE

Jin and Shakey at swift water school.

On a Sunday afternoon I rode my Harley over to Station 1 to find out Jin Lee's impressions of Shakey. The apparatus doors were open, and I walked into the apparatus room. As I open the kitchen door, Captain Trussel asked, "What are you doing here, LO?" (That is the name a lot of firefighters called me.) I told him I was writing a book about Shakey and needed to talk to Jin Lee. Cass (Williams) was working on lunch, a big sheet pan of nachos, that he was about to put in the oven.

Jin came in from the living room after hearing me talking about Shakey and greeted me. I asked, "Do you want to eat first?"

He said, "No, I want to do this." We walked into the captain's office and Jin closed the door. For the next hour, I hear a younger firefighter's thoughts on what it was like working for Shakey.

Instant Hero Status

"When were you hired?" I asked Jin.

"In 2009, and like a lot of rookies I went to Station 2. There I immediately began hearing stories of this legendary firefighter called Shakey. Lieutenant (Hugh) Harris was always talking about him. He told us about Shakey flying to Spain and running with the bulls. I thought, *this is the kind of captain I want to work for*. I was always thinking, *I would love to go to One's and work for him. He had instant hero status with me*."

I Get My Chance

"I was falling into the busy routine at Two's and enjoying being an Irving firefighter. We made a lot of calls at Station 2. But I wasn't an EMT (Emergency Medical Technician) and needed to be. So halfway through my probation, I had to take care of that. Grant Blake taught ECA (Emergency Care Attendant), and it was a 40-hour class that I had to do before the department sent me to EMT school. After I completed EMT school, they sent me back to Two's to finish my probation period."

"Then, low and behold, a hole opens at One's. Cass had torn his ACL skiing and needed surgery. The department sent out a temporary transfer list and I saw my name on it. I'm going to One's! I had got my wish to work for Shakey. With me still being a rookie, it was a good move for me. Engine 1 was the only engine in town, at that time, who had a four-man crew. With so little fire experience, I could lean on these more experienced firefighters who had fought a lot of fire."

"The day came for me to report to One's, and after putting my fire gear on the engine and checking my SCBA, I go help with cooking breakfast. We had fried eggs, bacon and sausage, hash brown potatoes, and biscuits. I put a couple jars of jelly, honey, and orange juice on the table. As we sit down to eat, Shakey comes out of his office and sees me and says, 'Lee, finally a name I can pronounce!' That was the first thing he said to me."

Two Fires That First Day

"After breakfast I start cleaning the house, sweeping the floors, mopping, start cleaning the bathroom, and the tone goes off. We are dispatched to a structure fire. I race to the engine to bunk out (term for putting on our fire 'bunker' gear). I see that Shakey has already climbed into the cab. As we are driving, I'm excited, trying to look and see if we have any smoke showing. Shakey tells Dispatch 'We have a little smoke showing.' I'm now really excited. I get off and Shakey says, 'Wait here. I'm going to see what's in the backyard.' He knew the fire was small by the amount of smoke. It turned out to be a greenhouse in the backyard that was burning. He radios for me to bring the reel line, as he disregards the other fire equipment. We knocked the fire out pretty quickly, load up all of our equipment, and head back to the Station from my first fire with Shakey."

"Later that evening we had a huge fire on the edge of Station 5's district and Station 1's district off Hunter Ferrell (Road). Up till this time in my career, the only real nozzle time on a structure fire was the live burn training at Dallas-Fort Worth (DFW) Airport." Pointing at me, Jin says, 'You've been there and done that, captain. It's a simulated fire with natural gas. It's dark and hot inside the building, but it isn't like a real fire, right?' (DFW fire crews' control when the fire would be extinguished by turning off the gas.) "The only other fires I had were a couple of large two-alarm apartment fires, but Engine 2 wasn't first in on either of these fires. I had some nozzle time on both of these fires, mainly putting out spot fires. So, this is my first real fire where I was the initial attack crew."

"I grab a hose line with Shakey, and we head for the house. I feel the line stiffen as Joe Carey sends us water. We were pulling the line toward the house with my heart racing. As we near the front porch, Shakey yells for me to knock the fire down that is engulfing the porch. It was roaring out the front door. I opened the nozzle and started fighting fire like we had trained at DFW. Shakey immediately corrects me and begins telling me what to do. Then we start crawling our way up the stairs of the porch and inch our way inside the house ... fighting fire. Here Shakey is, 70 years old, and he is right there beside me telling me what to do the whole time." I could hear him plainly, cause he never connected his regulator to his mask."

"After a long battle we extinguish the fire. Other crews are mopping up. We are sitting in Rehab, but Shakey won't sit down, going around telling us all what a good job we had done. I'm exhausted, but he's wanting us now to go help with overhaul. There was a lot of damage to the house, so it took a while before we got back to the station. But I knew right then that this was going to be my home, Station 1, working for Shakey."

Isn't This Great?

"When I was at Station 2, I made it my goal to try to be the first one on the engine for every fire call. So that was going to be my goal at Station 1. Here, the first fire I had, Shakey beats me to the engine. He did that on most runs we had, up to the last day he worked. Even when we made a run at 2 or 3 o'clock in the morning, he would get up and beat us to the engine."

When a firefighter hears that we have a structure fire, we race to the engine, step in our bunker pants, pull them up, grab our fire coat, put it on, climb in, strap on our SCBA, and buckle ourselves in, while our Driver puts his headset on, starts the engine, flipping on the emergency lights, and pulling out of the station, not knowing what kind of formidable opponent we will face. There is nothing like that, adrenaline pumping through your veins.

Jin continues, "Then through the headsets we would hear Shakey say, 'Guys, isn't this great?' Almost on every run we made he would say that. He loved being a firefighter."

Language Pay

"Shakey also liked the fact that Jorge (Castro) and I were there to interpret on medical calls. I am fluent in Korean, and Jorge spoke Spanish. One's district is a very diverse district with many Koreans living in it. Both of us being bilingual were a big help on our medical runs. What was ironic for me is that the city wouldn't pay me language pay for Korean, even though I used it often.

"The city offered a class at North Lake College to learn Spanish so we could communicate with our patients. Me and about fifteen others attended the class. We would go when we finished our shift. I was able to pass the speaking part of the test at the end of the class. I now receive language pay for Spanish, but can't receive pay for Korean, even though I'm fluent in it.

Go figure."

Coloring Outside the Lines

"When I first got here to One's, all of my crew helped me a lot. One of the first stories they told me about Shakey was a call they made and how he would handle things ... kinda his way. The story was that they had just sat down to eat dinner, hot food straight from the stove left on the kitchen table. You know how it is, captain, they had to go make the call. The call was an arcing power line. They got there and Shakey radioed Dispatch and asked for the power company to come out. The line kept arcing and they couldn't leave until the power company came and fixed it.

One of the crew members, his name will go unsaid, was getting impatient, wanting to go back to the station and eat. So Shakey grabbed a long pike pole (mainly used to pull ceilings down so you can fight fire). They said that Shakey whacked the arcing line, and it fell on the phone line below it, causing it to catch fire. Shakey called Dispatch and told them that the telephone line is now on fire and to call the phone company. The phone company got there quick, of course, to restore the telephone service. With them being on scene, it allowed the engine and crew to go back to a cold dinner. They told me this story to show me how

Shakey handles things differently than a lot of the other officers. And, of course, he did.

"Each Fire Station has its own culture, mainly because of who the captains were. When I was at Two's, we were very much a 'strictly by the book' Station. One Station functioned totally different. Shakey would look at the situation and see what was going on, then make a decision. Sometimes it bounced a little outside the line of the department policy, but we would do the right thing at the right time to help the public.

"For example, we had a shooting call. Dispatch told us to stage and wait for IPD [Irving Police Department] like they always would. We staged a few houses down from the address, and Shakey saw this man who we had run on before. He was sitting on the ground and there was no one around him. And no IPD! He told Joe, 'Pull up there and see what's going on.' As we were walking up, you could see he had been shot in the butt, probably from a drug deal gone wrong. Shakey yells, 'Where is the guy that shot you?' To which the guy said, 'He is gone.' IPD is now there. We packaged him up, and the ambulance takes him to Parkland (Hospital). The next shift we get another gunshot call, and Dispatch warns us three times to stage. Maybe we did. Maybe we didn't. Shakey always did what he thought was right at the time.

"He taught all of us that when we make a call on a person, make that person feel special, no matter who they are. Make them feel we are here for them. Shakey did that all the time. Even when driving back to the station, he would see someone with a flat tire and stop and help him change it. Or if he saw someone that looked down on his luck, he would have the driver pull over and Shakey would talk to them. Then we would see Shakey opening his billfold and giving that person some money. Sometimes all the money he had in his wallet."

Last Thoughts

"He was a mentor, a father figure, a brother, a granddad to my kids. He taught me what is important in life. Family! I had the idea that my job was to provide for my family. As long as I was doing that, it was alright.

"My oldest son was a good hockey player and played in college. My wife took him to all the practices and games. I thought if I paid for it, I was doing my part. That's what made me a good husband and father. And I had it completely wrong. Shakey would tell us, 'You have to spend time with your kids.' I saw that in him. How important family is to him. He encouraged us to bring our families to the Station. Shakey would come to my son's hockey games. We would go to Nimitz (High School) on the engine and watch his grandson's team play. His grandson was the baseball coach. He encouraged all his men to do this. He would say, 'Make sure you are taking care of your family.'

"Being a firefighter who got to work for Shakey, I'm so thankful. He helped me to shift my mind to where my family is now my main priority. I'm so thankful that Shakey showed me and taught me by his example. I would have missed a lot with my oldest son by not working and learning from Shakey. I became a better person and father. I'm still at Station 1, teaching these new rookies what Shakey taught me: how to treat people and their family, the way Shakey treated people."

MATT SMITH

I sat down with Matt and asked, "When did you first meet Shakey?"

"I joined the department in January of 1987. There were 17 of us in my rookie class. We were hired to open Station 9. Everyone had heard of Shakey. I worked at Station 7 with you for several years. Then I went to Station 3, and I met him a couple times. Shakey was at One's and that's when Chief Hickey let us play volleyball during the day. So, they would come to play volleyball once in a while, but he and I never really talked.

I had promoted to Driver, and I knew Chief Ray and Doss (Battalion Chief) were thinking about sending me to One's, or (Robert) Downey. So, I went down to One's and went into the Station and told Shakey I was interested in driving for him. Shakey said, 'If you are campaigning for the spot, I want you down here.' So, I went downtown and saw Chief Hickey and told him I would go to One's.

My transfer was March of 1995, and I was his Driver for 11 years. Only Don Burrows drove for him longer than me. Jim Caudle was there, and we were in rookie school together and Randy Yowell was the other firefighter, so the transition was real easy. All I had to do was to get to know Shakey—and it didn't take long."

40 Years of Service

Matt continued, "I knew that Shakey's 40th year on the department was coming up. I felt like that was a big deal, and I got the guys together and organized a party at the Station. The other shifts pitched in some money, and I got a plaque made up for him, and we had a party for him. I felt that he deserved to have that kind of treatment for serving (the department) that long. That really impressed Shakey, and we instantly became friends. It led us to have annual parties at his house, going to Ranger games and other things.

When Shakey married Ginger, they had me and my wife over to their house for dinner. My wife and Ginger hit it off immediately. We started having bigger parties and Shakey got some of the old guys there to meet some of the younger guys. They would tell us all about the old stories that had happened. It was always a good time. We had these parties every year until COVID."

Never Met a Stranger

"What impressed me the most is how Shakey never met a stranger. Whenever you were around him, he always put people at ease. He also was always helping someone. Once there was a young guy out front of the Station. Shakey saw him and we went out to see what the matter was. The guy told him he was having a hard time. Shakey ended up buying him lunch and some other things. We never saw him again, but that is how Shakey is, always helping people.

Many times, we would go on an ambulance call with 523 or 525 (how we identified an ambulance from Station 3 or 5 in those years). We would treat the patient and the ambulance would haul them off to the hospital. Shakey usually knew someone there or he would stay and talk to family. Shakey would still be talking and me and the tailboard would hear the ambulance clear the hospital and most of the time we would hear them check back at the Station. There Shakey was, still talking. We would be thinking, '*Let's go Shakey.*' He might be talking to them about something that happened way back in the sixties.

One time during the divorce we were on a call and Barstow was tailboard. He finally got tired of waiting and got up in the cab of the engine and grabbed what he thought was the mic for the *intercom*. He said, 'Ruby is back at the Station getting your stuff.' Dispatch responded, 'Engine 1, do we need to send IPD?' With a big laugh Matt told me, 'Barstool had grabbed the mic for *dispatch*.' That's how Shakey was, he never met a stranger."

Shakey's Leadership Style

Chief Brunacini of the Phoenix Fire Department was one the most highly respected figures in the fire service. He was invited to come to Irving to speak to the department about his leadership style. Shakey and his crew were on duty that day. They stowed their gear on the engine, and Shakey radioed dispatch, 'Injun One, clear, to go to The Arts Center for a talk.'

"The lecture was on customer service in the Fire Service. Brunacini taught about servant leadership … customer service … be nice … treat everyone like you care. Shakey was doing that way before Brunacini ever wrote his book. I think that was Shakey's leadership style. That's what we did at Station 1 A shift. Just go help all people no matter what time it was or who they were.

When we got back to the station later that morning, Shakey said, 'what that guy taught us was simple stuff. People should do that all the time. It's common sense.' Working with Shakey, we saw him do that all the time. Even when he was off duty, we saw how he helped people."

On the Nozzle

"Shakey trained his men. He wasn't like other officers, who wanted the nozzle when they had a fire. He let us take the nozzle. He was training his men to fight fire, letting them be first in on the nozzle. Going into a fire, he hardly ever connected his face piece. You could hear him clearly talking, telling a firefighter what to do and how to attack a fire.

Another thing he did, that always worried me, was he went into fires without his gloves on. I would get on him about not wearing his gloves, but somehow, he always came out unscathed. Shakey always said *we* are going to do this. It was always *we*. Whatever *we* did, he participated. Shakey never gave us orders to do something; he participated with us, at the Station and on the fire ground. Yowell, a lot of the time would complain about things we had to do. He finally realized and said, 'Why should I complain? Shakey's been doing this for nearly 50 years?'"

Always Teaching

"When Mike (Worthington) came to One's, we had a big apartment fire. We were doing a primary search, kicking in doors and making sure everyone was out. Shakey kicked a door open, and Mike said, 'Let me kick the next one.' Mike kicked the door and his foot went through one of the panels. It was one of those six panel doors. He was stuck, hopping up and down, trying to pull his foot out. His boot wouldn't let him. We were helping him get his foot out, and Shakey said, 'You dumb butt; kick it close to the doorknob.' Shakey rarely, if ever, cussed. About the worst thing he would say is to call someone a dumb butt. On the next-door Mike kicked in the right spot like Shakey had taught him. Shakey was always teaching his men, always teaching. He wanted us to learn something at every incident."

Not What It Looked Like

"Once we got dispatched to a grass fire. When we pulled up, we saw this big bushy tree on fire. It was a real cold night and I told Shakey, 'Stay in the cab, we got this.' So, I got out and got us some water as Cass (Williams) pulled an attack line. We were putting the fire out and I began to wonder, *where is Mike*? I said, to myself, *He must be talking to Shakey, making us do all the work.'* We worked our way around the tree, and there was Mike doing CPR on this big guy. The man had driven his truck up into this tree and it was about four foot off the ground. Mike had gone around the backside and pulled him out. He must have weighed 300 pounds, and the (radiant) heat was really hot. I helped Mike pull him further from the fire, as Cass fought the fire. Shakey got out and was helping us and called for an ambulance. We loaded him and they took him to Parkland (hospital). He didn't make it, but it was one of those unique situations that we all learned from."

Like a Brother to Me

Matt ended our conversation with this story. "My family over the years did a lot together with Shakey and then with Ginger. We went on many family vacations together. My kids grew up with Shakey and Ginger. When my oldest son was getting married, he asked me if Shakey would fill in as a grandfather. My dad was in a nursing home, and he couldn't travel. So, we went and asked Shakey if he would fill in for my dad. Of course, Shakey agreed. He was part of my other kid's wedding, too.

When I asked my mom about him being in the wedding, she said, 'It was alright. He has been like a father to you.' But I told her, 'No, he's like a brother. I had only one dad.' That's how close me and Shakey are. My mom even recognized the relationship we had had all these years. Even though he is a lot older than me, we are brothers."

Matt Smith promoted to the rank of battalion chief, retiring after serving the citizens of Irving for 36 years, Shakey also gave him one of his bronze statues.

A job well done, Matt!

RONNIE MAYO

Driving down a narrow street in south Irving, between the cars that lined both sides of the street, I stopped in front of Ronnie's house, and I immediately noticed perfection. Walking up to the front door, I'm still admiring how immaculately the yard is kept. I rang the doorbell and Ronnie opened the door. He greeted me with a firm handshake and welcomed me. He introduced me to his wife, Barbara, as they sat down on their couch, and I sat in the recliner beside them. I noticed that the inside of the house is even more perfect than the outside. And so was the hour I spent hearing stories about the Irving Fire Department and Shakey Holder.

Wanting to Be Rich

"When did you buy the house?" I asked Ronnie.

"We bought it in 1963, for $9,000," replied Ronnie. The three of us laugh at the thought of a house costing $9,000. Ronnie continued, "I served in the Air Force in England and was a firefighter in the military. I met my wife there, and we were married in 1963. I went to work for the City of Irving in the water department with Jerry Gammill, Don Burrows and Ed Violet." With a wry smile he says, "We made $200 a month. I was good friends with Johnny Sargent, and his dad heard the fire department was hiring for the new fire station (Station 5). This was 1967. So, the four of us went and took the test. All of us passed and were hired. Bear Bryant, Kenneth Heine, and Gunter were also hired off that test. Now working for the fire department, we are making $400 a month, double what we were making at the water department. We all felt like we were rich. We always said if we had $10,000 in the bank, we would be rich."

Beginning a Career

"I started my career at Station 3 with Captain Lee Pollei and Grider. We called Grider, Hunk. I worked there for a while, and a new transfer list came out. I was going to Station 2. So, Pollei and Hunk started setting me up. They were telling these big stories about Shakey and how he was and how he was really hard to work for. They said the first thing he is going to do was to get me to box him. So, I decided right then, that I wasn't going to take no crap off of him."

Respect

The day came for Ronnie to go to Two's. "Driving there I keep thinking what Pollei had said to me ... how hard it was to work for Shakey. I walked into the station, and I went straight to Shakey and said, 'captain, I've heard all about you, and I'm not going to take any of your crap.' Shakey, taken aback, says, 'What do you mean ... OK ... OK, that's all right.' That's how mine and Shakey's relationship started.

"Then the next shift was a Saturday and sure enough he wants to box me. Shakey, walking to the bedroom, says, 'We are going to box and there's no hitting in the face.' We put the gloves on and the first thing he did was hit me hard in the face. But it didn't take me long to learn to respect the man and we became good, lifelong friends."

Going to Court

"Shakey and I were working at Station 2, and the engine and truck catch a fire. We bunk out and pull out on Story (Road) headed North. The light at Irving Blvd. is red, but we run the light. I'm standing up, putting my gear on, and to my right I immediately see a car coming, and he is not stopping. I brace myself as the car hits us, in the side of the engine. Shakey radio's dispatch and tells them we were in a wreck and to send IPD. We go and talk to the man who hit us and to see if he is alright. He's really mad and yelling at us. A man walks over from the store at the corner, where the Arby's used to be, and the guy in the wreck says to the guy, 'Did you see that fire truck run the red light?'

The guy said, 'No, I saw a stupid SOB hit a fire truck.'"

"We get back to the station and Shakey says that the man is going to sue us. I say, 'How can he sue us? He hit us.' Shakey was right! Two weeks later we are in court being sued."

Getting His Mind Right

"Bull Durham drove for Shakey at Station 2, and I was his tailboard. Bull was always a cautious Driver, and it drove Shakey crazy. He would drive like he was driving his car. He would stay in his lane behind the other cars when we were running on an emergency call. Shakey wanted him to split the center line and make the cars pull over to the side of the road and let us get by them.

"One day we get a run to Bear Creek. Bull is driving like he always did, and Shakey is yelling at him, wanting us to get to the fire as fast as we can. Shakey had brought this thick limb from a tree and had it beside him in the cab of the engine. Bull wouldn't do what Shakey wanted him to do, so Shakey grabs that stick and whacks the top of the hood hard. (In those days the city bought equipment that didn't have a roof over the cab. They would saw them off. We were told it was for better visibility. What it wasn't good for was cold winter days or rainy downpours.) When Shakey whacked the hood, it scared Bull almost to death, but from then on he drove like Shakey wanted him to."

Real Men

"These men who worked in the early years of the fire department were *men*. Many of them served our country in war. Most, if not all, were from humble means. They worked hard to provide for their families both at the station and at their part-time jobs. They didn't want to work with anyone who they thought was weak. They needed someone who could hold their own in tough situations. They tested you. They wanted to see if they could count on you in hard, dangerous situations. If they saw a weak chicken, they would 'peck it to death.' They also played hard, both off duty and at the station. They were always pulling pranks while they were on duty to see how you would react. It was the culture of the fire department in those days."

During my interview with Ronnie, he didn't talk a lot about fires he fought. He talked about the pranks that he saw and participated in at the station. Most of us, who were a part of that generation and their pranks, are now retired. We have a new generation that gets the job done, without the shenanigans of those early heroes.

Frozen Shoes

"When I worked Saturdays, I would bring my dress shoes to the station and polish them when I did my duty shoes. When I finished shining my dress shoes, I put them by my bed to take home the next morning. We also had to clean the chief's office every Saturday. After breakfast I slid the pole to the apparatus room and filled a mop bucket with soap and hot water, while the other guys cleaned the kitchen. Moss came down and we were sitting in the chairs in front of the station watching the cars go by. Jimmy (Cox) slid the pole. We heard a racket, turned around, and saw him stomping in the mop bucket with his shoes on. We started laughing, until I saw it was my new dress shoes. I go to grab him, and he runs to the back parking lot and kicks my shoes off.

"Well, now I'd have to defend my reputation. So that night I get up to go pee, and I quietly get Cox's shoes by his bed. I go to the kitchen and fill them with water and put them in the freezer. Next morning, he gets up and sees his shoes are gone and yells at me, 'Where are my shoes?' All the guys are laughing and looking to see what I've done with them. We tussled for a minute, and I tell him to go look in the freezer. They are frozen solid." With a laugh Ronnie says, "He had to drive home in his bunker boots."

Don't Look!

"We started building dune buggies and racing them. We belonged to a club in Grapevine, and our families would go out on the weekends and camp out and race our dune buggies. All our boys became friends and learned to drive by racing each other. But my story about the dune buggies and Shakey started one Saturday at Central (Station). Jimmy Cox could weld, and Shakey had bought a new Volkswagen. We were cutting it up and Cox was welding it back together. He told Shakey to watch how he welded. So, Shakey, wanting to learn how to weld, was staring. When Cox would strike an arc to weld, Shakey was watching. Cox is welding, and Shakey is staring right at the bright light. We all knew that this is going to burn his eyes, but no one stops him from looking at the weld.

"We finish building for the day, and I go home. Shakey is on duty, so he finishes his day at the station and goes to bed later that night. The next morning, they all get up and see that Shakey is not there. His bed is made, but he is not in the station. They go to the dispatch office and ask,

'Where is Shakey?' The guy dispatching says, "Shakey's eyes were hurting him so bad he had to go to the hospital."

They played hard in those days.

Other Pranks

"Shakey had a sub one Saturday. Bobby Butcher was working for him. He liked cars and after breakfast we went out to take a look at my new car I had just bought. It was a used Thunderbird. He noticed that I was missing one of the hubcaps. They were those chrome spoke spinners. They looked really nice on the car. Bobby said, 'I got a guy that could probably find you one.' I asked if he would call him and see if he could find me a hubcap. We went inside and Bobby called him. Bobby comes out of his office and tells me the guy had some. I ask how much? Bobby said he wanted $15 for one. I told him I would give him $15, to call him back. He calls him and Bobby tells me, he can be here around 3 o'clock.

"Sure enough, he comes to the station with this nice hubcap. I thanked him and give him the fifteen dollars. We all walked out to my car, and I shake his hand again, thanking him. All the guys are out there, telling me what a good deal I just got, as I pull the rear fender skirt off. I put my new used chrome hubcap on and step back admiring it. And the guys kept telling me how lucky I was, that Bobby was here today and that he has so many friends in the car business.

"Then one of the guy's yells from the other side of the car, 'Mayo, someone has stolen one of your hubcaps.' I run around the back of the car and look ... *they got me good on this ONE.*"

Water Is Important for Firefighter

"Shakey was the captain at Central (Station) and Epperson was his lieutenant. I was assigned there along with Harold Montgomery and Moss. It was a good crew, and we worked well together. After supper we usually would slide the pole and get our chairs and sit outside and watch the cars drive by in front of the station. People would drive by and wave at us. Sometimes people would stop and ask directions or just talk. We would just sit out there and smoke ... most nights ... waiting to see if we got an (emergency) call.

"Montgomery had just lit another cigarette and was leaning back in his chair against the apparatus door. I noticed this car that had been waiting at the red light, looking up and pointing. The light turned green, and they are driving real slowly in front of us, still looking up. Then all of a sudden, a bucket of water hits Montgomery on top of his head–hits him perfectly, with only the filter of his cigarette left in his lips. Water splashes us also, but we are laughing our butts off. And so are the people in the car, as they honk and wave and then drive off.

"What had happened, Epp had a five-gallon bucket in the back of his truck. He and Shakey got it and filled it with water. They had climbed up on top of the station with the bucket of water, and Epp hit Montgomery perfectly with it."

Part of a Family

"The thing is, you don't get mad at pranks. You just have to laugh and pay them back when you get your chance. Montgomery didn't this shift, but I'm sure he got even some way. But several times it got way out of hand. We had times when they would go start the engine and pull a reel line into the station and wet everything trying to get even with someone. When you heard the pump engage, you knew you were in for a long day or night. Many times we would have to put our mattresses on the (fire) hose rack and let them dry out so we could sleep on them that night.

"You are part of a family. We spent more time with the guys working 24-hour shifts, than with your own family. It was always better if you worked together and were a family. It was fun then. Shakey ran his station differently than a lot of the other captains. He expected you to do what he asked, and he would be right there with you doing whatever chores we had to do. If you didn't, you had trouble with him. He also wouldn't give you a lot of busy work, like other captains did who had their men just doing busy work all day. He wanted you to know your job, your equipment, know your district. Just do what was expected and necessary. If you did that, you wouldn't have any trouble with him. He treated you like family."

Last Thoughts

After about an hour of sitting and listening to Ronnie's stories, with his wife by his side and both of us laughing at Ronnie's stories, I ask, "What final thoughts do you want to say about Shakey?"

Ronnie without hesitation and with a deep breath says, "Greatest person in the world."

There was a long pause, as I contemplated what he had just said. Looking at him, I ask, "What do you mean by that statement?"

Ronnie says, "If he knew you, he would be there for you. If you needed money, he would give it to you. He was that kind of person. Once he had a bet with Wendell McClure, and Shakey won the bet. Pooh [his nickname] wrote him a check and handed it to Shakey. He never cashed the check. I bet he still has it. Once, he and Ginger went to England on vacation with Chief Knopf. He made a special effort to go find the town my wife was from and see it. It blew us away that he would do that. He made everyone feel he really cared about them. And he did care. I could tell you a lot more stories like that … greatest man I've ever met."

CALVIN MORRIS

Sometimes you receive a special gift at the right time. This happened to Shakey while we were nearing the completion of this book. He received a call from someone he had not heard from in over 20 years. His name is Calvin Morris. He is now 51 years old. I called Calvin and this is their story.

Calvin grew up in a biracial family in the 70s. He was born out of wedlock, and his mother married an African American man. Life was hard for them in those years. They grew up poor, and his parents wanted to move out of their South Oak Cliff apartment in Dallas and rent a house in Irving. Calvin's stepfather called several numbers who had a house for rent, and no one would rent to them, because he was African American. Then they saw a *for rent* sign on 110 Collins Street, Shakey's first home he bought. Calvin's 15-year-old brother called the number from a pay phone outside their apartment and lives were changed forever.

Are You Serious?

Shakey rented them the house, and one day drove by and saw Calvin riding his motorcycle up and down the street with his brother. Shakey stopped and told them about his sons, riding their motorcycles up and down this same street. Calvin told Mr. Holder (Calvin always calls him Mr. Holder) that he bought the motorcycle with the money he earned mowing lawns last summer.

This impressed Shakey and he asked Calvin, "How old are you?"

Calvin answered, "Twelve."

"I have some rent houses; you want to go to work for me?"

Calvin excitingly says, "Sure, I've been working in Honey Grove (Texas) remodeling a house. I like working."

"I'll pay you $5 an hour."

"Are you serious?"

He was being paid $2.50 an hour in Honey Grove, and the minimum wage at that time was $3.25 an hour. He thought, *I'm going to be rich*!

As Shakey was getting to know Calvin, he asked, "What do you like to spend your money on?"

"Coke," Calvin answered.

"Wait a minute, you're too young to being doing that."

"No, no, Mr. Holder, I mean Coke like Dr. Peppers."

That story has stuck in Calvin's mind all these years, and when he finished the story, he got choked up. It lasted around 30 seconds with complete silence. After gathering his composure, he apologized and said, "I owe everything to Mr. Holder."

Calvin continued, "He would pick me up from school after football practice, take me to work for two or three hours with him, and then drive me home. I loved it because the walk from school to home was about two miles. I got paid and a ride home! Sometimes he would take me to lunch. I told him that I was too dirty to go out to eat. He said, 'We have money; they'll let us eat.' He would take me to Cheddars, or my favorite, Angelo's. It was a real treat for me to eat in those places and listen to Mr. Holder.

"Another thing I remember ... my parents were at least three months behind on our rent. I told Mr. Holder he shouldn't be paying me while my parents owe him money. He said, 'That has nothing to do with you; that's your parents' problem.' I saw a lot of people do him that way, not paying their rent.

"He would call me Caloboy, how Shakey must have said cowboy and would always say, 'Caloboy, you got to work like you live, hard and fast.' He's not the type person who is going to be sweet and nice to you, talking to you like a baby. He's going to show you how to make good decisions and live life. No fluff. Mr. Holder means a lot to me. I never had a grandfather. He opened my eyes to how to be successful. He was a friend, a savior."

Choking up again, he whispers, "He means so much to me."

What Are You Doing Now?

I asked Calvin, "What are you doing now?"

He answered, "I work for Dr. Pepper as a merchandising manager. I have seven supervisors under me and 135 employees. I supervise my employees the same way Mr. Holder taught me. I speak of things he taught me to my employees at least every couple of months. I have a good life, two kids, who are all doing well. I never thought I would have the life I have, if it weren't for meeting Mr. Holder, I wouldn't have."

Mr. Holder

About an hour after our interview, my phone dinged, and Calvin had texted me this message:

"Most people may know Mr. Holder as Shakey and a firefighter. Mr. Holder was much more to me than his profession. I called him Mr. Holder and always will. I always respected Mr. Holder too much to call him anything else. I, without thinking twice, would not be the man I am today without his influence. My kids are adults and amazing, only because of the life skills Mr. Holder taught me. They know of Mr. Holder but may not realize Mr. Holder taught me how to be a good person, father, and provider for my family. Mr. Holder was a grandfather, father, friend, and mentor I needed in my life. I think of him often and speak of him to all my family and friends whenever I get a chance. One of the many things he taught me was work as hard as you live. Never forgot him encouraging me to work hard and fast while he was holding the ladder steady when I was painting. I would sometimes not use enough paint. He said, 'Paint is cheap. Labor is expensive. Put more paint on the brush.' So many amazing memories, it was not work for me, it was spending time with him, learning and getting overpaid. Honestly, I would do that part of my life over many times but would ask for no pay. The world would benefit from his life experiences."

Yes, they would, Calvin!

THOUGHTS FROM THE HEART

What you are about to read are the emails I received expressing the heartfelt words of love and gratitude from the heart of family, close friends and firefighters who have been enriched with the unconditional love and wisdom of the man they call Grandad or Shakey.

JOSH HOLDER,
SHAKEY'S OLDEST GRANDSON

W hen I was asked to write something about Shakey, or Grand-dad as I called him, my first thought was, *where do I start?* Maybe I should tell stories about my first memory playing in the mud in the yard on Manana, shortly after he and Ruby first moved in; but then that brings up the memory of finding the electric car that Shakey had hidden under a dozen blankets in the garage that was supposed to be a surprise for me. Or maybe I should share my memories about all the motorcycle riding on the Honda Mini Trail I watched him rebuild, or driving his boat, or going on trips, or working on rent houses, or being scared to death walking through the woods by Lake Texoma in the middle of the night to find some old pirate ship boat in a pond that Granddad thought he had seen, it was really there by the way.

My mind just starts to race through all the things I got to do growing up with Granddad. By the time I was 6 or so, I was sitting on his lap driving his truck. Then six years later I was driving myself, following him home about 60 miles from picking up some old car from a shop in Oklahoma. Driving with Granddad was probably one of my biggest memories. He let me drive everywhere. Legal or not, he didn't care. Come to think about it, I remember driving down the new section of Highway 75, North of Denison, before it was opened to the public. I asked, "What if we get caught?"

He just replied, "We will just tell them we are going down here to talk to one of the construction workers."

Just an example of how we made our own rules back then. See when you are with Granddad, you are larger than life and nothing can hurt you; and that feeling is still the same today. What I love about him the most is the sense of protection you get when you are around him. I can only imagine the relief people would feel, seeing him show up in his hero suit when people called the fire department for help. Regardless of if he knows you or doesn't, you can bet your last dollar he is going to protect you. He is everyone's hero. I think that is what his purpose is in life. I believe he was gifted to this world to save the people that need it and be a benchmark for the rest. In all my life, I have never met a man that has his level of motivation. After all, he worked for 56 years for the community, 19 years at his second job, and created a rental business while doing all his own repairs and maintenance.

All this, and still had time to make you feel special, to make you feel like if you slipped up and needed something, he has enough care and motivation reserved just for you. He always puts everyone else first, and honestly, I have never seen him ask for something in return. My most favorite quote from him, and I use it a lot to this very day is, "If you need anything, you let me know." Nothing describes Shakey better than that. That is what he told me right before he drove off the day, I purchased my first home.

So, when asked to say something about Granddad, what I want to say is, "Let's be like him. Let's make him proud and carry on his legacy of not asking but doing. Just like him, we are put here to provide a service to the world and protection for those around us. That is how we can repay him for all that he has done." Overall, my most favorite thing to do with

Granddad is "pal around." That's what he called it when he would ask me to go somewhere, or just come over, when I was a kid. There is no better feeling than to hear those words. Any moment with him is like being on top of the world, and I am proud to say I get to live in a world with Shakey!!!

AUSTIN JEFFERY,
SHAKEY'S GRANDSON

To most he was known as "Shakey," but to his beloved grand-children, he was simply "Granddad." Granddad is a remarkable individual, a hero in his own right, having spent his working years battling flames and saving lives. However, the true heroism in his life was the love and devotion he showered upon his grandchildren.

Every summer, when school was out, it was an unspoken tradition that my brother and I would pack our bags and head over to Grand-dad's place. Sometimes it was for a couple of days and other times it was weeks. It was kind of like our mini vacation. He owned a house with a beautiful backyard and a sparkling pool, the perfect sanctuary for his grandchildren. Those summer days were a paradise created by Grand-dad's love and generosity.

The mornings were always special. We would get up early, and together with Granddad, prepare a hearty breakfast. There was some-thing special about sharing this simple meal, and the warmth of the kitchen filled with the smell of pancakes and sizzling bacon. We would laugh, make a mess, and create unforgettable memories.

After breakfast, it was time to embrace the sun. Granddad had a rule: no electronics by the pool. He wanted us to savor every moment, and so we did. The pool was our kingdom, the water our playground. Granddad, in his faded swim trunks, would sit by the pool, watching us with a twinkle in his eye. He would toss footballs high into the air, and as we jumped into the pool to catch them, we felt like we were the best receivers on NFL Sunday. Those throws symbolized more than just a game; they represented the love, trust, and encouragement he offered to us.

Lunch was a simple affair—sandwiches and lemonade. We would talk about our dreams and Granddad would listen attentively. He would tell us stories of his time as a firefighter, instilling in me the values of bravery, selflessness, and service to others. His experiences were a source of inspiration, and his wisdom became my guiding light.

The summers with Granddad were not just about poolside fun. There was another side to the adventures—the rent houses. Granddad was a handyman, and he owned several rental properties in the area. He often needed a hand with maintenance and repairs. During our visits, I became his eager assistant. Granddad had a special way of teaching. He would patiently show us how to fix a leaky faucet, repair a broken step, or paint a room and sometimes the entire house. "Put some paint on that roller," he would always say. I learned to use tools and gained the confidence to tackle household projects.

With each summer that passed, I became more skilled. I picked up plumbing, carpentry, and electrical know-how. I learned how to install a fan, lay down flooring, refinish a floor that had been flooded and other skills that I will continue to use as I grow older. Whenever we stopped for a break, or made a Home Depot run he would always leave his tools scattered amongst the rent house. I would always ask if he needed to lock up, and his response was always, "if someone needs it more than me, they can have it!" I watched and learned as Granddad demonstrated the art of problem-solving, something that would serve me well in the future.

Evenings were filled with laughter and delicious dinners. Which mostly consisted of more pancakes and bacon. There was just something about breakfast for dinner that made it taste better! Granddad, with a twinkle in his eye, would boast to anyone who would listen about the wonderful grandsons he had, who not only knew how to have fun but also had the skills to maintain his rental properties.

As I grew older, I realized the immense value of the lessons learned during those summer projects. The skills I acquired were more than just handyman skills: they were life skills. I learned about responsibility, hard work, and the satisfaction of a job well done. One of the things Granddad would always say was, "if it's not done perfectly, it's not worth doing!" These lessons were the seeds of self-reliance that would grow and flourish in my adult life.

Now, I look back on those summers with immense gratitude for the remarkable man who not only saved lives as a firefighter but also enriched mine with love, wisdom and the most treasured memories. Granddad's legacy will continue to live on, not only in the lives he touched as a firefighter but in the hearts of his grandsons who will forever carry his love with them and utilize the valuable skills Granddad blessed us with.

JULIE GAUTHIER MARQUETT, GINGER'S DAUGHTER

If you ever met Shakey Holder, you will likely never forget him. He is well respected, accomplished and maybe a bit stubborn. He is a remarkable man. My family and I are blessed to have him in our lives.

ROBBY GAUTHIER, GINGER'S SON

After my mother's divorce from my father, all I could think about was her being happy. When she met Gene, I felt like he was the one for her. After dating him for six months, she said, "I'm not sure if he's serious." I said, "Mom, give him another month." Finally, after three years, he stepped up to the plate. They've been happily married ever since. They are a true inspiration of love. My mom deserved a superhero, and she got one in Gene, out of all eight billion people in the world. I think they found their soul mates. They both are inspirations. I couldn't have asked for a better stepfather, or partner for my mom. He's always been a hero to me. I'm grateful for him every day.

After I graduated with a Bachelor of Science in Sociology/Psychology from Texas State University, I worked in social work for 10 years, first as a wilderness counselor, and then a director of Parent Children Services for Kilgore Crises Center in Texas. There I wrote a million-dollar grant, which funded our program for four years. Then I became the director of admissions and program director for Azleway Children Services, still one of the largest providers in Texas.

All the while, thinking about being a fireman like my superhero step-dad Gene. I took the fireman's test in 1999 and scored 95 and didn't qualify for military/police extra points needed to get in. I ended up going to Hollywood and getting into SAG-AFTRA (still a union member after 21 years.)

I still wish I had pursued being a firefighter. It's truly one of the most superhero jobs out there, and my stepfather Gene is the best. He's the oldest line fireman ever, still doing swift water rescue at 79, still passing the physical tests. He's got a day named after him in Texas ... look it up. He is a superhero! I'm proud to call him my stepfather, and I'm so grateful for the happiness he's given and continues to give my MOM. Thank you, Gene, you're awesome! I love you! You deserve to have your superhero story told!

NICK HOLDER,
SHAKEY'S GRANDSON

Every time I go back to Texas, Granddad likes to tell the same story about me as a child. I would swear I have heard it a dozen times. It's about a bunch of young kids on a golf course near his house. We are walking with him along the path, nearing a dark tunnel that runs under the course.

He decides to play a practical joke on us. He warns us there are tigers in the tunnel ahead. To hear him tell it, I didn't buy it for a second. I bravely, confidently told him there aren't any tigers in the tunnel, and I walked right in. That is the way he saw me in that moment—unafraid, self-assured, and assertive. Beyond that moment, he sees that in me. It is a story he can tell that shows who I was as a kid, and a part of who I am now.

I never saw myself as that brave, confident kid. But that's his magic— the ability to see things in you that you can't always see yourself. He sees those faint glimmers of goodness or strength and brings them out. He makes you see it too. It is why he has never met a stranger and how he makes everyone feel welcome.

Maybe his stories are a little bit larger than life sometimes. I'm pretty shy, not particularly confident at times (quite the opposite of the boy in that story), but I know I have that brave, self-assurance in me too. He reminds me of that every time I go home.

KAGAN DUFFY, SHAKEY'S GRANDSON

Billy Gene Holder or as I lovingly call him, Granddad, has been a pivotal role model for me my entire 31 years on this planet. From a young age, Granddad has instilled the importance of hard work into me. I remember as a kid he would take me to his rental property to clean them from top to bottom before new tenants occupied them. I didn't realize it then, but as an adult I value the lessons he taught me through those experiences. Diligence, perseverance and being intentional and purposeful with everything I do, only touches the surface.

He also taught me that family is everything. One of my fondest memories of Granddad is the regular sleepovers my cousins and I would have at their house. We would swim and play all day, and in the mornings, we'd be greeted with a giant spread of breakfast food. I wouldn't trade those memories for anything. I find myself to be so lucky to have such loving grandparents in my life and my son, Jaxson's, life. I don't know where we would be without their love and support. Granddad is the first person to call me when I mess up, but he is the first person to recognize my accomplishments. We love him so much.

KELLY MARKHAM, FAMILY FRIEND

I can count on one hand the number of people I trust implicitly, and Shakey Holder is one of them. His membership in this small club is unique in that we're not related by blood, profession, or childhood friendship. I'm a former girlfriend of his stepson, and when that 13-year relationship was in its death throes, I told my then boyfriend, "The two of us are breaking up, but I'm not breaking up with Shakey or Ginger." I could accept the end of the relationship, but losing Shakey and Ginger was unthinkable.

I've known Shakey for over 20 years now. I liked him the moment I met him, struck by his kindness and warmth toward someone who was a total stranger to him. Through the years, I've been a witness to the unshakeable values and moral code that make Shakey who he is. These include his generous spirit, honesty and integrity. His eagerness to help anyone who is struggling. His refusal to give up when things get difficult. His dedication to work, both as an extraordinary firefighter and as someone who values work as essential to a happy and satisfying life. For Shakey, cleaning the gutters or working on one of his rent houses is a fine way to spend a Saturday.

My life has been touched by Shakey in so many ways. He has always been unfailing, supportive, kind, and generous. He once drove eight hours to deliver a washer, dryer and sofa to our spartan apartment after my boyfriend and I relocated to Jackson, Mississippi. He made multiple trips to Los Angeles to visit us, driving thousands of miles round trip and yet refused to even let me pick up a dinner check. And once when I was scared and desperate and unsure where to turn, Shakey stepped in and set things right. I didn't ask him to, and I didn't expect him to, but he did.

GARRET JEFFERY, SHAKEY'S GRANDSON

It is such a great honor to be able to write a piece in a book about the life of the most honorable man I have ever met. He has made an impact on so many lives, and there has not been another person with a greater impact on mine. My first memory that I have is with my Granddad, and I will cherish that one, along with every other memory in between, for as long as I live.

I could probably fill a book up with all the lessons and memories that involve him, but I will focus on what I consider the most valuable lesson, which came from my teenage years when I helped him on his rent houses. Even though I was a teenager, my Granddad, in his late 70s, outworked me every day. I do not believe he was more physically able, but because of the attitude he chose to have. In 100+ degree heat, he might have been more physically tired than me, but it never showed, and he never let whatever level of tiredness he may have felt affect his quality of work.

He enjoys working hard; he enjoys doing things the right way, and probably more than anything enjoys using the aforementioned to help and get the best from those around him. Being able to see and experience that firsthand has allowed me the ability to emulate that attitude at work and at home, and I will eventually try to pass that on to my own kids and grandkids. Nothing makes me prouder than making my Granddad proud, and I will continue to try to do so for the rest of my life.

JIM CAUDLE,
IRVING FIREFIGHTER

When I first got assigned to Station One, my immediate thoughts were, *I was scared*. Shakey and (Don) Burrows were two of the older guys in the department. I thought these two old guys are going to get me killed. But when I got there and started to work with them, I had never felt so secure as I did working with them.

Shakey and I immediately became buddies. He had just been served his divorce papers, and I was single. We pushed the boundaries; that's for sure. He is my second dad. I would do anything in the world for the man. It was my biggest honor, working for him and a pleasure knowing him. He is one of those rare people to have in your life.

RONNIE YANKEY, RETIRED CAPTAIN, IRVING FIRE DEPT.

The Irving Fire Department has several certified specialty teams in addition to their Fire Fighting and EMS duties, such as HazMat, Urban Search and Rescue and Swift Water Teams. When the Department added the Swift Water Team, Ronnie knew the demands of the training and went and talked to Shakey about the class. "I told Shakey all about the demands of the training since I was one of three who were first certified in swift water, but Shakey didn't want to leave his Station and was threatening the Department with age discrimination if they didn't let him go. I frankly thought the class was too tough for Shakey. It was in New Braunfels on the Comal River that flowed through town and into the Guadalupe, but the department sent him. He was in his mid to late 60s, too.

This class was the most demanding and dangerous class I had attended. The class began at eight in the morning until five o'clock in the evening and half the time was spent in the river, training. The first thing we had to do was a forty-yard swim in the river without a floatation device, which was pretty tough. We were also, in Landa Park, which had a spillway and it had eroded holes over the years where it empties into the river, that would suck you under even with a PFD (personal floatation device). You would have a victim you were rescuing and go through the chute and try not to get sucked under. It was dangerous. We even had a night search in the Guadalupe, where it was dark, and you were looking for victims.

It was serious training and Shakey did every one of the evolutions. He did everyone and never quit, just like Shakey always did. What he did in his career is amazing. He was just like me … he did what he loved … being a firefighter.

AMANDA,
SHAKEY'S GRANDDAUGHTER

My grandfather is the definition of "you can do anything you put your mind to." He is a vastly powerful and intelligent man. While he may be stubborn and hardheaded from time to time, he always means well by his words and actions. I know that without his headstrong attitude and kindness, I would not have grown into the woman I am today. I am very proud to get to call him my grandfather and be his only granddaughter.

EARL YARBROUGH,
FRIEND

My name is Earl Yarbrough, and I grew up next door to Pistol Mitchell, the first fire marshal for the City of Irving. I was starting into my freshman year in high school and wanted a summer job. I talked to Pistol and he said he had one of the firemen named, Shakey, that he would talk to about a job for me. Well, I had some baggage. I had polio at the age of two in one leg, which slowed me down a little, but needed a chance to prove myself. Shakey was that person. I have told this to many people in my life about Shakey; he was the first person to hire me. And the first person to fire me as I smile and laugh about the story. Shakey is one in a million to do what he has done. Shakey to be an active fireman for 56 years is unbelievable. That is two full-retirement careers back-to-back.

My senior year when I graduated, he brought me in that summer and said, "I'm going to let you go. I know you are planning to coast and I'm not going to let you. It's time for you to get out of your comfort zone, working here, and find a career." I tried talking my way out but to no avail. He had his mind made up. I was heartbroken and left. I have to say looking back Shakey knew best. It was less than a year when Pistol asked me if I would consider working in a pawn whop. His nephew, Jack Daugherty, started Ace Pawn Shop and was needing help. I worked for Jack for five years. Jack later started the chain of pawn shops called Cash America, which is the largest chain of pawn shops in the world. I started my own, working there for the next 39 years and retired in August 2017. Shakey had 56 years under his belt. What a guy! I have to say I have the utmost love, honor, and respect and call him a friend to this day.

DR. PERKINS,
SHAKEY'S ONCOLOGIST

I first met Billy Holder in 2005 when he was referred to me for further management of his chronic lymphocytic leukemia (CLL). He had been diagnosed with chronic lymphocytic leukemia in 2004. He has been on and off various medications for this, and it has been under reasonable control. In 2015 he developed a mass in the left neck from skin cancer and this was removed and followed by radiation. He subsequently developed squamous cancer on the left ear with a node behind the ear. He was treated with immunotherapy, but the cancer did not respond. He had surgery for the skin cancer and subsequently developed lung metastases. We treated him with a different immune therapy, and he had a complete response and has remained in remission for four years off treatment.

I have known Billy for a long time, and he is a great guy who never complains. Despite his age and against my advice, he likes to climb on roofs and ladders. He is also a landlord who has several houses but is clearly not cut out to be a landlord. If his tenants cannot afford to pay the rent, he just does not collect it.

I look forward to many more years of interacting with Billy and his family.

JEAN HICKS,
GINGER'S BEST FRIEND

I remember the day I first heard the name Shakey Holder. My BF had gone to defensive driving school and then went out with a group of friends after this to a bar. Shakey spotted Ginger in the bar, and the rest is history. Well, not so fast, there was a lot of history in between, even though Ginger hardly ever went to bars, she met her man there.

The relationship took off from there in hot pursuit and Ginger pulling back from time to time. Then the dance reversed; she wanted more, and he was the standoffish one. When they first got together, Shakey bought her a sofa for $500, and Shakey thought he got himself a hot chick that wasn't going to cost him all his money. Wrong again! They were going to a wedding, and Shakey asked me to take her dress shopping, and money was not an issue. We headed to Dallas to Lester Melnick and found the perfect dress for $700. He tried to act like it was nothing, but I'm sure he swallowed hard.

Shakey wasn't much of a drinker. Ginger and I back then did shots of Tequila. We didn't want the calories from mixed drinks. You probably needed to be there, but we had a couple of Tequila shots, but when

Shakey grabbed the Tequila bottle and took a swig and then took a full bite out of a whole lime and ate it, we laughed the rest of the night.

Shakey and Ginger were Charlie's and my greatest traveling companions all over Europe and the States. Charlie considered him BF, and our favorite restaurant was 3 Forks restaurant, where we shared many special occasions.

My children, Katherine and Michael, have always looked up to Shakey and thought of him as family. He was there for many of Michael's football games and then at Michael's son's football games as a Celina Bobcat.

Shakey is a giver, and he and Ginger helped Charlie and I throw many Christmas parties for over a hundred people that included drinks, live band for dancing. It was the highlight of our year.

A lot of people go through life never having the kind of friends Charlie and I had in Ginger and Shakey.

A Job Well Done!

ENDNOTES

1   Wikipedia, https://en.wikipedia.org/wiki/Urban_legend

2   THE IDIOMS, largest idiom dictionary

3   Oxford Languages and Google Dictionary

4   Wikipedia, htts://en.wikipedia.org>wiki

5   CNN.com, "8 of the most notorious Ponzi schemes in US history," April 24, 2021

ABOUT THE AUTHOR

Clif Clifton is not the name my parents gave me at birth, but a nickname I gave myself entering junior high school and somehow the name stuck. Living life on the edge of a "cliff" the past 68 years with no fear; by enjoying riding my Harley across the United States, 40 years serving others as a firefighter in Irving and Italy, Texas, and traveling the world on mission for the Lord the name now seems fitting. My joy for writing began with journaling, then writing poetry and now my first book. God has been good!

www.ingramcontent.com/pod-product-compliance
Lightning Source LLC
Chambersburg PA
CBHW071329120626
46546CB00002B/501